TO Rangada

from

Pikon

7.9.83

THE COMPLETE BEGINNER'S GUIDE

TO PHOTOGRAPHY

Other Doubleday Books by George Laycock:

ANIMAL MOVERS

THE CAMELS

PEOPLE AND OTHER MAMMALS

STRANGE MONSTERS AND GREAT SEARCHES

MYSTERIES, MONSTERS AND UNTOLD SECRETS

THE BIRD WATCHER'S BIBLE

THE PELICANS

THE COMPLETE BEGINNER'S GUIDE to PHOTOGRAPHY

by
George Laycock

DOUBLEDAY & COMPANY, INC.
GARDEN CITY, NEW YORK

Library of Congress Cataloging in Publication Data

Laycock, George.
The Complete Beginner's Guide to Photography.

(The Complete Beginner's Guide Series)
Includes index.
SUMMARY: Discusses the selection and care
of cameras and equipment,
techniques of photography,
development of film,
and photography as a business.
1. Photography—Juvenile literature.
[1. Photography] I. Title.
TR149.L39   770'.28
ISBN: 0-385-13264-6 Trade
0-385-13265-4 Prebound
Library of Congress Catalog Card Number 78–1207

9 8 7 6 5 4 3

CONTENTS

THE COMPLETE BEGINNER'S GUIDE
TO PHOTOGRAPHY

1. THE BEGINNING PHOTOGRAPHER

When you return from the camera shop and open your package for a first serious look at your new camera, you join the largest of all groups of hobbyists. There are millions of cameras. Through them run miles of fresh film every year, and out of them comes an endless display of pictures, both color and black-and-white.

Cameras can enrich your life. They catch the images of friends and relatives in pictures that will become family treasures. They capture moments you want to remember and record, the high points of your travels. They are also important because there is a real sense of satisfaction in making a picture.

Remember that your new camera doesn't know anything. Even if it is one of the more recent "automatic" designs, it is not going to take a single picture by itself. Only one thing makes it a valuable picture-taking machine—you.

When the camera, even the fanciest one, goes to work, it gives an impersonal reaction to what it sees. Wheels move, little doors open and close. Everything it is pointed toward is of equal importance. If you make a picture of a glamorous movie star walking past a garbage can, the movie star and the garbage can get equal billing from your camera. Again, it is the photographer who makes the difference.

Much of the pleasure of photography comes from controlling the way your camera records subjects. Photography becomes creative in this way, and reflects the thinking and feeling of the person behind the camera. True, anyone today can take snapshots. Point camera,

Family activities make excellent photo subjects. This picture of father and son will bring back memories years later. (*Photo by the author*)

press shutter, and you've taken another photograph. The whole process has been made so simple that many people think there is no longer any challenge to it. But the challenge is there, and always will be, for anyone who wants to create photographs that rise above the average.

The surprising discovery is that most of us, by simply following some basic rules, can improve our pictures greatly. Instead of turning out another batch of ho-hum snapshots, we can create pictures that will put us into the ranks of the better-than-average photographers. From that point, we can go on studying and improving as long as we like.

Photography is a major influence in our lives. We see pictures every day in newspapers, magazines, movie theaters, television programs, and on billboards. Photographs have become so much a part of our lives, it is difficult to imagine what the world would be like if film and cameras had never been invented.

The story of cameras goes back a long way. Hundreds of years ago people learned that an image coming through a tiny hole in the side of a tent or building makes an upside-down image on the opposite wall. Eventually, scientists learned that silver salts are sensitive to light. Then they learned to coat surfaces with these salts and capture images striking them through a lens. The development of negatives followed, so the photographer could make as many pictures from a single negative as he or she wanted. Then came roll film late in the 1880s, and with this invention, photography was off on its race to become the world's favorite hobby.

But it is more than a hobby—far more. Among the earliest photographers whose work was important for recording history was Mathew B. Brady, who photographed battle scenes during the Civil War. Shortly afterward, photographs made in Wyoming played an important part in the creation of our first national park: Yellowstone.

Today photography continues to grow. Cameras are vital to business and industry. Cameras record developments in laboratories and field research stations. Professional photographers travel to every corner of the earth to make pictures.

Meanwhile beginning photographers read, enroll in classes, and join clubs to learn about cameras and how to use them better. The beauty of photography is that it does not have to be a costly hobby. Excellent pictures can be made with simple cameras. This is proved every day by beginners, working to make each picture the best they can with whatever equipment they own.

2. CHOOSING A CAMERA

THE SIMPLEST CAMERAS ON THE MARKET do not have to be set. They have one lens opening, one shutter speed, and a fixed focus. Some of these are even programed to take pictures in dim indoor light. They can turn out good snapshots, and they may be as much camera as some photographers will ever need.

But serious photographers will soon find that they want a different kind of camera for making a wider variety of pictures. Many photographers, both beginners and professionals, like the modern single-lens reflex cameras. The SLR camera has a mirror on the inside. When you look into the viewfinder, the image toward which the camera is pointed passes through the lens, reflects into the mirror, then up into the viewfinder. The mirror is behind the lens, where it would block the light coming through the lens and keep it away from the film. But at the instant the exposure is made, the mirror flips up out of the way, then flips down into place again. When you are taking a picture, you are not aware of this mechanism because the mirror moves with such speed. The big advantage of a reflex camera is that you see exactly what you will get on the film.

If you are going to buy an SLR camera, it is almost certain to be a 35mm. This designation refers to the size film it takes. The roll of film has perforations along the side, and these holes fit into sprockets in the camera. The sprocket wheels pull the film through the camera, moving the exposed piece of film out of the way and advancing the next frame for the next picture. The size of a 35mm frame of film is about 1"x1⅜".

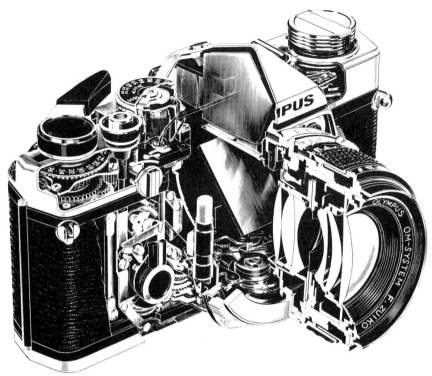

A cross-sectional drawing showing some of the working parts of a 35mm SLR camera. (*Vivitar Corporation Photo*)

This seems very small, but it is big enough for a careful worker in the darkroom to make sharp enlargements from, if the image is sharp to begin with. Most black-and-white film of this size can make sharp enlargments in the standard 8x10 size or even 11x14.

This is why few people need a camera larger than 35mm. A majority of professional photographers today, including newspaper camera people, carry 35mm cameras. In addition to being compact and easy to use, they are versatile and can handle almost any kind of photographic job.

There are also reflex cameras with two lenses, one above the other; these are called twin-lens reflex. They are still used by both professional and amateur photographers. Although there is a mirror in the twin-lens camera, it does not move. It can stay in place behind the upper lens because it does not block light from the film. The only function of the upper lens is to let the photographer see the image.

The two lenses are positioned so they both point at exactly the same thing, and in this way the photographer knows what is in his picture as he shoots it.

Most twin-lens reflex cameras are made for 120 roll film. There are either twelve or twenty-four exposures on one of these rolls, and each one makes a negative two and a quarter inches square. Their advantage over a 35mm is that there is a larger negative to work with. But these cameras are generally heavier than the 35mm SLRs and have to be reloaded more often. If you want to shoot color slides, the 35mm size is a better choice, because most projectors are made to handle only 35mm pictures. But if you come across a good buy in a larger twin-lens reflex and want to work mostly with black-and-white, it might be a good camera for you.

Also figuring heavily into the choice of a camera is whether or not it can be fitted with different lenses. Less expensive cameras normally have one standard lens, and no more. Other cameras, however, are made so that you can easily remove a lens and replace it with a different one.

This feature adds to the cost, because a camera that will take a va-

A typical single-lens reflex camera, one of many brands widely used by both beginners and professional photographers. (*Braun North America Photo*)

riety of lenses is a more complex machine. Most of us, when choosing a camera, have to think about cost. There is also the matter of how the camera will be used. If, for the most part, you want to take family snapshots and occasional pictures of your friends, you may not need a camera with more than one lens. In this case, get a simple camera that is easy to use and inexpensive. You can still do your own developing and printing if you want to. But you will be limited in the variety of pictures you can take. A simple camera with one fixed lens will not allow you to shoot those distant scenes you can get with a telephoto lens. If you are not likely to be taking such pictures anyhow, a simple camera may be your best choice.

On the other hand, if you think you may someday want to become more deeply involved with photography, it is better to start out with the best camera you can afford.

This does not mean that you will have, or need, more than one lens right away. The beauty of this plan is that you can add a new lens, or other piece of equipment, as money becomes available. A solidly built camera, well cared for, should last many years; this is why you should buy the best one you can afford in the beginning. It will become the foundation of all your photographic equipment.

Consider also whether or not any of your relatives or friends have cameras with interchangeable lenses. If they do, you may want to buy the same kind. Then you can own different lenses and pool your equipment. In addition, if you should buy a second camera, it is an advantage if they are both alike so that all lenses and other attachments are interchangeable.

A secret to holding down the cost of a camera is to choose one that will do the jobs you want without a lot of extra features you would use rarely, if ever. For example, some cameras are equipped to set shutter speeds electronically. The camera automatically adjusts itself to changing light conditions. This is handy, but not essential. A less expensive camera may have one or two needles which you line up in the viewfinder to get the right exposure. These take a little more effort on the part of the photographer, but they work perfectly well.

Lens "speed" can also play a big role in the cost of photographic equipment. You may buy a "fast" lens that opens up to $f/2$ or $f/1.4$. Then you may find that you almost never open the lens all the way. You could save money by settling for a slower lens. If, however, you will frequently make pictures in dim light, you may need the fast lens.

The right choice boils down to figuring out what you will really need, then trying to match a camera to those needs.

INSTANT PICTURES

Among the most remarkable cameras ever invented was one introduced by Edwin H. Land in 1947. Land's Polaroid camera not only made the picture but also developed it, like a camera and darkroom all packed into one. Besides, the picture came from the camera completely developed and ready for viewing in less than a minute.

At first this invention was not taken seriously. People had once said of the first airplane, "It will never fly"; now they were saying the same thing of Land's unbelievable camera.

But the new invention offered features people liked. The photographer could get a quick look at his finished picture without waiting for the roll of film to be completed, then waiting longer while it was developed and prints were made. Instead of days or weeks, the picture could be seen in seconds, and if it was not good, the subject could be photographed again.

This instant photography was possible because the inventor of the revolutionary camera had worked out a method of packing printing paper and chemicals together inside the camera. At first, the new cameras could turn out only black-and-white pictures. But instant color photography was then introduced by the same firm. A different camera and special film made it possible to make both a black-and-white picture and a negative by this method. Even professionals, in growing numbers, began to use Polaroid cameras.

If you are thinking about a first camera, however, consider also what one of these cameras will *not* do for you. If you want to do your own darkroom work, you will do better to consider another camera system. If you want to make slides for use in a projector, you will also need a different camera. Most photographers who take pictures for publication also rely on standard cameras and darkrooms for making most of their photographs.

But Polaroid Land cameras are still growing in popularity, and we probably have not yet seen all the new ideas that will grow from that first startling breakthrough in 1947.

In 1972 Kodak brought out the 110, a compact camera made to fit in the pocket. It used 16mm film. Within five years the public bought 50 million of them. The 110 is the most popular camera on the market, and several manufacturers now produce them. There are several reasons for their popularity.

First, they are easy to use. Manufacturers advertise that you can "just point and shoot." Most of their features are automatic. They do not have all the adjustable features of the larger 35mm cameras. Instead, they are pre-set at a fixed *f*/stop. They may have two shutter speeds and be equipped with automatic flash. Some are offered with more than one lens, so their owners can switch from a close-up to a telephoto lens.

In addition, the 110s are about as easy to load as a camera can be. Open the back, drop in a film cartridge, close the back, that's all. They are lightweight and handy, just right for the person who does not consider himself or herself a photographer, but still wants a camera for trips and family gatherings.

These 110s are most often used for making pictures that will come back from the processor as color prints measuring 3½″x4½″. They can also be used for making either slides or black-and-white prints. The negative is much smaller than a 35mm, however, and for this reason it is more difficult to get a sharp enlargement that is not objectionably grainy. Its light weight can make it difficult for some people to hold this little camera steady. If you are interested mostly in black-and-white prints, a 35mm camera would be a better choice. The 35mm is also better if you want to do serious photographic work using various lenses under a wide variety of conditions.

There are also pocket-sized 35mm cameras which, although larger and heavier than most 110s, are small and compact enough to fit in a pocket or purse. The final choice of a camera hinges on cost—how much you think you will use a camera, how serious you are about photography, and how important the size factor is. The thing to do is survey all the possibilities, then make a choice to fit your own purpose.

The stores today are filled with cameras in confusing variety. There is strong competition among manufacturers. This leads to all manner of "improvements" and a constant parade of new equipment. Some photographers become so caught up in the search for the "best" camera that they never learn all they should about any camera. The fact is that the photographer is more important than the camera.

An outside and an inside look at the modern pocket-sized camera. The Kodak Tele-Instamatic 708, using 110 film, is one of numerous such cameras available. This model has a telephoto lens. Normal pictures are shot through an *f*/5.6 lens with a focal length of 25mm. By moving a switch on top of the camera, the photographer can slide a four-element converter lens into position to combine with the normal lens to form a lens of 43mm for telephoto pictures. (*Eastman Kodak Company Photos*)

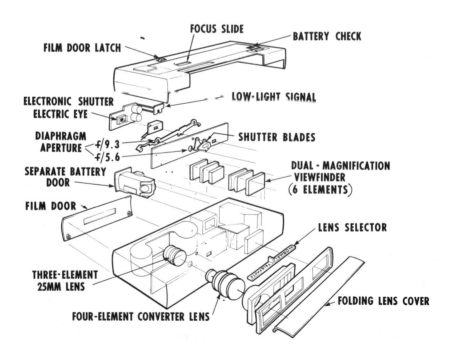

The Kodak Tele-Instamatic 608 camera, shown here with disposable flashbulbs attached, features two built-in lenses. (*Eastman Kodak Company Photo*)

New cameras are often purchased just before the owner leaves on a vacation trip. It's better to select and buy the camera a couple of weeks ahead so you have time to get accustomed to it and learn how it works. Strange things can happen. Mirrors can fail to flip up out of the way. Lens shades, which are attached to the front of the lens to keep out unwanted light, may be too small and cut off the corners of every picture. The shutter or diaphragm may not work correctly, and result in under- or overexposures.

But if you have time to run a test roll or two through the camera before leaving on your trip, you will know if everything is in order. While you are getting accustomed to your new camera, and before loading it with your first roll of film, study the directions that came with it. Even if you already know a lot about cameras, this is a good plan.

When you leave on your trip, carrying the new camera, take along the instruction book. It takes very little room in the camera bag. Questions may come up, and the booklet should give you the answers.

3. A LENS FOR EVERY JOB

BEFORE DISCUSSING WHICH LENSES you should have, let's take a look at what a lens is and how it does its job.

The lens is the eye of the camera. It directs reflected light rays from the subject to the film. It is much like the human eye, except that what your eye does automatically and perfectly, the camera lens accomplishes with pieces of glass. The art of lens grinding has come a long way. Although today's camera lenses are no match for the human eye, they are still remarkable precision instruments.

Perfectly good pictures can be made with simple cameras that have only one lens permanently mounted. But as you become serious about photography you will probably want to advance to a camera with interchangeable lenses. Each of these will have a different *focal length*. Focal length is measured in millimeters. A lens may be a 55mm lens, a 28mm, 200mm, or any one of many others. Either the 50mm or 55mm lens is considered the normal lens on 35mm cameras. On cameras using 2¼ -inch-square film, 80mm is a normal lens.

Focal length is the distance from the lens where the rays of light passing through it converge when the lens is set at infinity. In addition, the lens has an *f* number. This number tells you the diameter of the lens in relation to its focal length. An *f*/1 lens has a diameter equal to its focal length, and an *f*/2 lens has a diameter one half its focal length. The greater the diameter of the lens, the more light it admits; this is why an *f*/2.8 lens is capable of making pictures in less light than an *f*/4.5 lens could when using the same film.

Close-up photography is possible with the addition of inexpensive elements to a regular lens. (*Photo by the author*)

Automatic lenses for 35mm SLR cameras and telephoto extenders. (*Bushnell Photo*)

When you use a telephoto lens on your camera, you increase the size of the image of any object seen through the viewfinder. This means that there is no longer room in the viewfinder for all you saw through the normal lens. The longer the lens, the narrower the field of view it will see.

If the lens is shorter than the 50mm on a 35mm camera, it is known as a wide-angle lens. Popular wide-angle lenses for the 35mm camera are 35mm and 28mm. Many professional photographers use a 35mm lens as their normal lens on a 35mm camera instead of the standard 50mm or 55mm.

The gray squirrel is a common resident in many cities, and a telephoto lens helps capture its portrait. (*Photo by the author*)

There are advantages and disadvantages to both short and long lenses. Each has its special jobs. The telephoto lens magnifies the subject. For this reason it is especially useful for photographing sporting events, taking wildlife pictures, or for candid shots of people from a distance. Short telephoto lenses, such as a 90mm on a 35mm camera, are also excellent for portraits. But while the telephoto lens magnifies the image, it also magnifies camera movement.

Telephoto lenses are normally long and heavy. One of the newer developments is a telephoto lens equipped with a system of mirrors. They are shorter and lighter than standard telephoto lenses. The mirror lenses, however, have only one f/stop setting, often f/8. Light is controlled by the shutter speed or by the use of density filters that reduce the amount of light striking the film.

Most people who buy telephoto lenses do not use them as often as they thought they would. But there are times when no other lens will get you as close to the subject as you want to be. At those moments the telephoto lens is the only way to get the picture.

Wide-angle lenses are useful for making pictures inside buildings, boats, automobiles, or anyplace else where the photographer wants to get maximum subject matter into the frame. They also give great depth of field, which is the area from the camera to infinity that is in focus. But distortion can become a problem.

Each lens has its job, and professional photographers carry a wide variety of them. Whether the assignment is a close-up of an insect, the inside of a hospital operating room, or a distance shot of a speedboat, they are ready for it. They know, from experience, which lens will give them the best picture under any circumstances they face.

Beginning photographers, however, can seldom afford such a variety of lenses, nor will they need them. If you are starting out with only one lens, select a normal lens as your first choice. It will give satisfactory results under the widest variety of circumstances. It is good for outdoor scenes, people, parties, and pets.

The choice of a second lens is tough and depends somewhat on your major interests. If you want to take nature pictures of animals that are shy and likely to keep their distance, you will need a telephoto lens. A 200mm lens is often a sound choice at this stage. It will also be useful for shooting athletic events. Next, obtain a wide-angle lens, perhaps a 28mm. The lens collection can go on from there as far as skill and money permit. There are telephoto lenses of

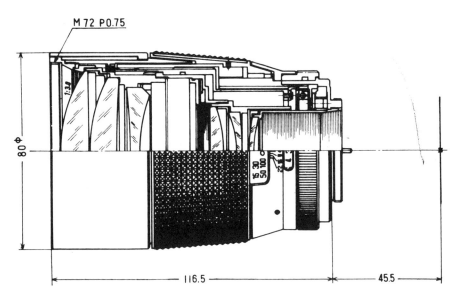

M 72 P0.75

80 Φ

116.5

45.5

A drawing showing the elements of the 200mm $f/3$ automatic telephoto lens. (*Vivitar Corporation Photo*)

An automatic 400mm telephoto lens for a 35mm SLR camera. (*Bushnell Photo*)

A 35mm wide-angle $f/2.8$ automatic lens. (*Bushnell Photo*)

A 28mm wide-angle $f/2.8$ automatic lens. (*Bushnell Photo*)

By changing lenses on a camera you can change the picture. These photographs were all taken from the same location but with lenses of different focal lengths, ranging from the wide-angle 20mm lens to the telephoto 500mm lens. Extra lenses are handy but not essential to making good pictures. (*Photos by the author*)

500mm and even 1,000mm. There are lenses with such wide angles of view that the photographer has to take care to keep from photographing his own toes when pointing the camera straight away from himself. They are all costly and their jobs are highly specialized.

There are also lenses known as "zoom lenses." By adjusting the lens with a slide-trombone action, the photographer gets a wide variety of focal lengths all in one lens. For example, one common zoom lens operates in the range of 80mm to 200mm. If you want to shoot a picture with a 150mm lens or 90mm, you have that too, without changing lenses.

An automatic 90–230mm zoom telephoto lens for 35mm SLR camera. (*Bush nell Photo*)

But the zoom lens may not be as sharp as the lens with a single focal length. This is especially true of the lower-priced zoom lenses. Before buying a zoom lens, do a lot of investigation. Talk with profes sionals who have used them. Try one out, if you can. A zoom lens can be a happy choice if you buy a good one, but a costly mistake if it gives you fuzzy pictures.

Light entering a lens must be under control. For a perfect exposure, exactly the right amount of light must reach the film. Light is controlled by two elements in the camera and lens—the iris diaphragm and the shutter.

The diaphragm is normally built into the lens. It is a series of small blades forming a flat disk with a hole in the middle, and as the blades move, the hole opens or closes. It can open as large as the lens, which is the largest f/stop for the lens. When we talk about the *speed* of a lens, we are really talking about the amount of light that is admitted through it. The more light it lets in, the better it should be for taking pictures in poor light.

The *f* numbers are marked on the lens. The smallest number refers to the largest opening of the diaphragm, which is the full size of the lens. On many cameras this wide-open setting is $f/3.5$ or $f/4$. The *f* numbers get higher as the blades close and the hole admitting light grows smaller. You can usually hear a slight click as the diaphragm reaches a new stop when you adjust the lens. Each stop toward a higher number cuts the amount of light by one half. At $f/11$ the lens admits half as much light as it does at $f/8$. Some inexpensive cameras do not have an adjustable diaphragm. The lens has only one speed.

Another control over the amount of light entering the camera is the shutter. In some cameras the shutters are built into the lens. But more often they are back of the lens inside the camera, right in front of the film. These are called focal-plane shutters. They are moving curtains with slots in them. These openings allow light coming through the diaphragm to reach the film. The diaphragm controls the amount of light that reaches the film, and the shutter determines how long it stays there. In expensive cameras the focal-plane shutter has various speeds. The fastest speed may be 1/500 second or 1/1000 second. The slowest will probably be marked B for bulb. When set on B, the shutter stays open as long as the button is held down.

4. FILTERS

BEFORE YOU'VE TAKEN PICTURES for very long, you will want to find out about filters. A filter is usually a disk of colored glass with a metal rim around it. The rim is to make the filter fit your camera lens. Because camera lenses come in so many sizes, you must make certain you are buying the right size filter. It should also have the kind of mount that will attach to your camera. Your camera store clerk can help you pick the right filter for your camera.

But there is still the matter of selecting the right filter for the pictures you hope to make. To do this you must understand what filters are for and how they work. At first this seems like a complicated subject, but let's trim it down to essentials.

Filters are made to adjust light quality and help the film do a better job of showing the subject either the way it is, or the way the photographer wants it to look in the finished picture. When the filter is attached to the lens, it makes changes in the light rays that pass through the lens and strike the film.

Keep in mind this rule concerning filters for use with black-and-white (panchromatic) film: The filter makes similar colors lighter and opposite colors darker. If the filter is green, it makes greens light. If there is a red canoe in your scene, the green filter makes the red print darker in the finished picture. If the filter is orange, it makes the blue sky, which is an opposite color, darker.

You will need only a few filters until you become an advanced amateur or a professional. Even then you will not often use a wide vari-

The photographer shot this action at the fastest possible speed, used a filter to darken the sky, and, in addition, was at the right place at the right moment. Practice and study can help anyone to make better sports action pictures. (*Canadian Government Office of Tourism Photo*)

ety of filters. There are three filters, however, that you should have. The most common filter used for black-and-white film is a medium yellow. It can be used to improve a wide variety of outdoor scenes, darkening the cool colors and making the warm colors lighter. It helps to make white clouds stand out against dark skies.

Another filter to consider for black-and-white film is green. This color is especially useful for outdoor portraits when using the sky as a background. The green filter makes flesh tones look more natural. It is also good for shooting flowers, because it makes warm colors stand out against either the sky or the green foliage around them.

A third filter to add to your set might be orange. It will do what the yellow filter does, but do it more dramatically. It makes water and sky stand out and sharpens textures such as stone and wood.

If you want to go a step farther, you might also buy a red filter. But red filters give such extreme contrasts that a picture of stormy-looking skies may look unnaturally dramatic. Any of the first three filters will have more general use than the red. The yellow filter can be kept on the camera for outdoor black-and-white pictures much of the time.

Remember when using a filter, that all color filters reduce the

This dramatic photo was made by a professional photographer, using a red filter to darken the sky over the swamp and to make jet trails stand out. (*Union Camp Corporation Photo*)

amount of light that reaches the film. This means you have to adjust exposure to let in more light to make up for the light the filter blocks out. Filters are usually marked with a "factor." If the filter is marked 2x, it means you must double the exposure time by opening the diaphragm one stop, because the filter cuts the amount of light by half. If it is a 3x filter, exposure must be increased one and a half stops; and a 4x filter, by two stops. A yellow filter normally has a 2x filter factor.

There are also filters made for use with color films. One is a haze (or skylight) filter. It has no filter factor and does not affect exposure times. It usually helps cut haze and makes colors look more natural by reducing blue reflections from the sky. Besides, it is an inexpensive way to protect the lens surface from dust and scratches. Many photographers leave this filter on the lens all the time for outdoor photography. But remember that the filter must be kept clean.

This Yosemite National Park scene is photographed thousands of times annually, sometimes well, sometimes not. Using a filter darkens the sky. A medium-fast speed catches some of the movement in the waterfalls. (*Photo by the author*)

You may also want a polarizing filter. These are expensive and can be tricky to use. They are used with both color and black-and-white film. There are situations where a polarizing filter can add much snap and drama to a color slide or a black-and-white negative. It can darken skies and reduce the reflection from water or other shiny surfaces. It also helps to cut through the blurring effect of haze. The polarizing filter is worth studying, then owning and using, if you are serious about photography. Some professional photographers who work outdoors most of the time say the polarizing filter is the most important one of all.

5. OTHER EQUIPMENT THAT HELPS

THE BIG JOB FOR A TRIPOD is to hold the camera steadier than the human hand can manage. If you hand-hold your camera while shooting pictures at lens speeds slower than 1/125 sec., you flirt with blurred or fuzzy pictures. True, photographers may get away with hand-holding a camera at slower speeds. But they are usually iron-nerved people with much experience. They know their capabilities, but they still blur a certain proportion of their slow-speed pictures. For this reason they use a tripod when time and conditions permit.

Tripods are available in considerable variety. Choose one to match the weight of your camera. A 35mm single-lens reflex camera does not need as much tripod under it as a large camera might. Besides, there will be times—in crowded rooms and places, where you must work fast—when a big tripod would be impractical. You will find yourself compromising between the size and weight when choosing a tripod that will work best for the kind of pictures you make. When comparing tripods, search for one that will fold up and can be easily carried, but still provide good camera support, even in a strong wind.

Check the tripod head. Some tripods have ball joints and tilt heads that allow the photographer to move the camera into any position he might want. On some, the center post can be removed and inserted upside down so that the camera is supported between the tripod legs for making close-up pictures of flowers or other objects at low posi-

Time exposures of evening or night street scenes make good subjects. This picture was made by using a tripod, and the only light was provided by the street lamp. (*Clarence W. Koch Photo*)

tions. The tripod legs should extend easily and telescope smoothly. When extended, the legs of some of the smallest tripods may be flimsy and bend easily under pressure.

No tripod is easy to carry, but some are small enough to fit into a camera bag. Others may fit a pouch carried on the belt, while others are so big they must be carried over the shoulder or in heavy luggage.

Another extra that goes with tripod work is a cable release for your camera. The pressure of your finger on the shutter release can move the camera enough to blur your pictures. The cable release is designed to eliminate camera movement. It is a cable-type plunger fitted into a flexible casing. Instead of pressing the shutter release directly, the photographer exposes the picture by pressing the plunger of the cable release. This can be done gently enough so that the pressure is not transferred from the flexible cable to the camera. It is one more bit of insurance against blurred pictures. And unlike the tripod, the cable release takes almost no space to carry.

When buying a cable release, be sure to get one that fits your camera and will not be in the way of the lens or moving parts.

As your collection of equipment grows, you will begin to look at those fancy camera-carrying bags in the photo shops. There comes a time when pockets are neither big enough nor handy enough to hold all your film, cameras, lenses, and other equipment. A good camera bag permits you to keep your equipment together. You can pick it up and be on your way without having to go through your room searching for each item separately.

The carrying case that may have come with your camera is good protection. If you do not have a camera equipment bag, you should keep the camera in its case.

The strongest camera bags are shaped like small suitcases and are usually made of aluminum. These are favorites with professional photographers. But they are costly.

A better choice for most nonprofessionals is a leather or plastic case equipped with a strong shoulder strap. The strap should be wide and padded so it does not cut into the shoulder. Check the clasp to

Choose a camera bag that will protect your equipment and is easy to use. If you carry only one camera and little extra equipment, you can get by with the case the camera came in. As you add to your equipment, you may want a bigger bag, even one that is waterproof for boat and beach outings. (*Photo by the author*)

see that the bag closes tightly against dust and rain. Most camera cases do not score high on this point.

The inside of the camera case should be lined with soft protective material. Elastic bands sewed into the case can help keep extra lenses, lens tissue, and film in place. Some photographers carry a few pieces of the plastic padding with built-in air bubbles that is used for padding fragile items for mailing. It is inexpensive and helps protect the camera from shock.

Your camera may not come equipped with a lens shade. If not, you should buy one. The lens shade cuts out reflections that can ruin a picture. It is especially valuable for making backlighted or sidelighted pictures. A good general rule is to keep the shade on the lens whenever you are using the camera. Some shades are made of flexible rubber so they fold flat for carrying. Check the shade to be sure it does not cut into corners of your pictures.

In addition, you should have a camel-hair brush or a puff bulb for the important task of keeping your lenses and filters clean. Keep a pack of lens tissue handy in case you have to remove an oily fingerprint from a lens surface.

These are the more common "extras" that photographers consider important even for beginners.

6. THE FILM

PHOTOGRAPHERS SHOULD UNDERSTAND what film is and how it performs its magic. The film that goes into your 35mm camera is a long, narrow strip of thin, flexible plastic. One side of it (the inside when the film is rolled) is coated with a tough, dried gelatin. Mixed into the gelatin are particles of silver compounds that are sensitive to light. This mixture of gelatin and silver is called the *emulsion*.

Some films have emulsions that are more sensitive to light than others. Less light is needed to change the silver compounds on fast films than on slow films. Films are given ASA numbers, which indicate how sensitive they are to light.

Medium-speed films range between ASA 64 and ASA 200, while fast films are those above ASA 200. With fast films you are better able to shoot action pictures or make photographs in poor light. But the faster the film, the more grain is likely to show in the print. Grain increases as you enlarge the picture.

Because of grain, many photographers settle for a good medium-speed film, with an ASA rating of between 100 and 200.

If you are having trouble making good pictures, the problems are probably not in the film. Films on the market today are carefully produced. Any film your photo dealer sells should do its job well. The important thing is to choose a film, then stick with it until you understand how to use it. The more you can standardize your choices of film, the easier photography becomes. Photographers often try to nar-

Using modern fast films, pictures such as this one, of a river towboat captain at work, do not need added flash. Pictures of people at work often make excellent and interesting photographs. (*Photo by the author*)

row their choices to a single kind of black-and-white film and one color film.

Film for 35mm cameras comes in either twenty or thirty-six exposures to the roll. If you have only one camera, there will be times when you have part of a roll of film in the camera but want to change to a different kind of film. There is no need to waste the rest of the roll of film. You can remove it from the camera, then later put it back and finish shooting the roll of film. All you do is wind the exposed film back into the cassette. But the instant you hear and feel the film

Indoor shots, such as this one, can be made with available light by using fast film, and, where needed, a tripod. (*Canadian Government Office of Tourism Photo*)

come off the spool, stop. This leaves the tab sticking out of the cassette so it can be reloaded in the camera. Make a note of the number of exposures already made on the removed roll. Later, when reloading the partly used roll into the camera, cover the lens while you advance the film to the frame it was on when removed. Then advance it three frames more. This way, you will probably waste only one or two frames.

7. BE GOOD
TO YOUR CAMERA

YOUR CAMERA CAN MAKE GOOD PICTURES for many years, maybe a lifetime, but only if you take good care of it. Cameras are precision instruments and are easily damaged.

Professional photographers often carry camera cases that are padded with foam. There is a good reason. The foam absorbs shock, and it cushions the cameras when the case is set down or bumped. Cameras and their equipment should be arranged so that they do not bang together in the camera case. When you haul your camera in a boat, or in any vehicle where there is a lot of vibration, set the camera case on a boat cushion or other padding to protect its contents.

Sand is an enemy of photographic equipment at the beach or in the desert. Strong winds can blow sand onto and into cameras even if the photographer is careful never to set the camera on the ground.

The tiny grains of hard sand can work their way into the camera's moving parts, where they can scar metal and destroy mechanisms. Anytime you adjust your camera and hear gritting sounds, stop working with it at once. Never force it. The more you move the parts, the more damage you can cause. Take it to the camera repair shop for cleaning.

One good way to protect equipment from sand is to keep a supply of plastic bags with you. These are especially effective if they come with wire ties or have self-sealing tops that close tightly. On the beach, where people are running and kicking up sand, it is good insurance to have all your film and equipment in such bags.

If you take your camera along on backpack or bike trips, keep two things in mind. First, you want to be able to get at the camera easily. It is too much trouble to dig it out from the bottom of the pack. If you pack it so that you can get to it easily, you are going to take more pictures. When you are backpacking, your camera is easier to get out if it is carried in a companion's pack so you can reach it without removing a pack from your back.

If you carry your camera on a neck strap, you can probably keep it under your jacket in case of rain or snow. Cameras carried on a strap during a hike, however, have a way of banging against the hiker's belly. This can be avoided by using a piece of elastic or a snap or buckle to fasten the camera to your belt. The longer the camera strap, the more the camera will bang around. Some photographers carry their cameras on a strap adjusted so that the camera hangs only inches beneath their chins.

Film needs special care too. It should not be left in the sun, near a radiator, or in other hot places. People often put their loaded camera or extra film into the glove compartment of their car, one of the worst places of all. As soon as the car is stopped in summer and closed up, heat begins to build, and heat changes the color in film. Film can be ruined if left in a high temperature. Heat can be especially damaging to exposed film. Black-and-white film is not so easily damaged as color, but it should also be stored in a cool dry place. Most modern films will stay in good condition at average room temperature, even somewhat longer than the expiration date printed on the package.

The more active the photographer, the more thought he or she should give to the care of camera equipment. The average camera case may not provide enough protection. Canoeists often want to take their cameras along on wild waters. If they do, they are likely to take some unforgettable pictures. But they may also dunk a camera, and a camera soaked once or twice is probably going to have to be junked. At best, it will mean a costly trip to the repair shop.

For this reason the canoeing photographer needs special protective gear for equipment. Some years ago it was possible to buy surplus military rubber bags that could be closed in a watertight seal. These may still be available in some places, so you may want to check nearby stores. Such bags should be small enough to be easily handled, but large enough to hold cameras, extra lenses, film, and perhaps food or a jacket. They should have webbed straps which can be buckled to

With care, cameras can be used in bad weather too—often to make pictures that tell a story. This canoeist turned one canoe up for shelter against the rain, and used the other for a lunch table. (*Photo by the author*)

a canoe thwart. Then, if the canoe flips, the camera bag stays with the canoe.

Wilderness supply stores and backpacking shops sometimes stock heavy-duty plastic bags that have air chambers. Cameras carried in these bags float if dumped overboard. Drawbacks are that these bags are fairly costly and do not hold much equipment.

Photographers have also used metal ammunition boxes for their cameras. These are watertight and so rugged they do not dent easily. They are inexpensive and can be purchased at military surplus stores.

If you travel by bicycle, camera equipment can be carried either in a day pack on your back or in saddle pouches on the carrier. Either way is easier than carrying a camera around your neck while pedaling.

Every camera case you use should have your name and address marked on in a manner that can not be rubbed or washed off. It is also sound practice to keep in a separate place a record of the serial numbers of each piece of photographic equipment you own. If your cameras are insured and you submit a claim, you will need the numbers. Even if they are not insured, police will need the information to recover stolen equipment.

KEEP THE LENS CLEAN

The single part of your camera that needs the most careful attention is the lens. It is a scientifically designed precision instrument and is easily damaged. Keeping the lens clean all the time increases your chances for making high-quality pictures. If you shoot through a dirty lens you will have problems making good prints once you start the darkroom phase of the process. This is why careful photographers always check the lens before taking pictures. (For the sake of the lens, the best cleaning is none at all. Keep it clean if you possibly can.) The lens is delicate. Keep a lens cap on it when not in use. The lens picks up fingerprints easily, and it should never be touched with the bare fingers. Its surface also attracts dust, which is in the air all the time almost everywhere. A small squeeze bulb will help clean a lens. So will a soft brush kept for the purpose.

If you watch photographers long enough, you will see someone take a handkerchief from a pocket and wipe the lens. You may even see the end of a necktie used to clean a lens. People who understand how delicate the surface of the lens is cringe because these rough cloths can scratch it. If the lens *must* be wiped, use a sheet of lens tissue. This is a special soft paper that can be purchased at any camera shop. But even lens tissues should be used carefully and no oftener than necessary.

If the lens still shows marks, use a drop of lens cleaning fluid, which you can also buy at the store, and wipe it dry with lens tissue. But use only the special tissues made for camera lenses. Some tissues made for eyeglasses are silicone treated. These should never be used on camera lenses or filters.

There are two basic rules to keep in mind always. Never force any adjustment on part of a camera. It should work smoothly. If force is needed to adjust it or fit parts together, something is wrong. Force will only make the repair more costly. Also, remember cleanliness. Whether in the field, studio, or darkroom, protecting equipment from dust and dirt gives you a better chance to make good pictures.

8. UNDERSTANDING LIGHT

MOST BEGINNERS do not give enough thought to light. With modern cameras you can get a surprising percentage of pictures that "come out." But if you want to make better photographs, begin by studying the properties of light and how you can use it or control it for your purposes.

Light is the raw material of which pictures are made. Cameras, films, developers, papers, and all the rest are only tools for using light.

Light travels. It moves from its source, which may be the sun, a lamp, a flashbulb, or a reflecting surface, at a speed so great that it is difficult to comprehend. In one second, light travels 186,000 miles. But the important thing is that, unless it touches something in its path, it travels in a straight line. If it bumps into anything, it may be absorbed or reflected. When we see an object, we see the light that is reflected from it. This is also what the camera "sees." By collecting this reflected light on a film, the camera records an image of the object.

Light creates shadows, and these are important parts of a picture. Shadows occur when an object blocks rays of light. If you photograph a sheet of white cardboard in the sun and it fills the whole frame, all of it evenly lighted, there is no picture. But if the shadow of your dog falls on it at the instant you expose the picture, you have an image because of the differences in light intensity. These differences, or shadows, may be in many tones from light to dark, or, as photographers say, soft or hard shadows. By controlling the lighting, you can soften shadows.

As an experiment, arrange some inanimate objects on a tabletop where you can photograph them at camera level. The objects should have shapes that give you a variety of shadow tones. Round vases, eggs, or a beach ball are good choices. Use black-and-white film and, if possible, use objects that are white or light-colored.

A melon photographed from two positions in sunlight shows how a slight change in camera position can bring out texture and form. In direct, flat light, the melon shows little detail. Placing the camera 90 degrees to one side adds depth to the subject and brings out detail. (*Photos by the author*)

Then make a picture with the sunlight falling directly onto the subject. Make three more pictures, each of them 90 degrees farther around the table. Two will be lighted from the sides, and one will be backlighted. When these four pictures are printed, study them carefully to see how shadows bring out form. What you learn about light from this and other studies can be applied to making pictures anywhere. The full straight-on light often makes a flat picture because there are few shadows. The backlighted one may be either a silhou-

Strong sidelighting makes an interesting picture of a camp scene in a Montana river canyon. (*Photo by the author*)

ette or a grayish picture that shows few details. The sidelighted pictures are likely to show the most interesting forms. Usually a picture taken at about 45 degrees to one side of the source of light will result in the best picture.

If you like studio photography, you can arrange lights for any number of variations on such a setup. You will want to make notes on each exposure so you can repeat those that please your eye.

The simplest way to carry extra light for your pictures is by including flashbulbs or a strobe unit in your camera bag. Flashbulbs are inserted in a holder with a reflector. When the bulb is fired, it gives a single bright flash, and it cannot be used again. In recent years photographers have been able to buy smaller and smaller flashbulbs, so they no longer have to carry around bulky packs of large bulbs. There are also flash cubes, which are sets of bulbs, each with its own built-in reflector, in a unit that fits into the camera. These are handy for the

Backlighting and exposing for the shadows make an interesting shot of campers preparing a meal. (*Photo by the author*)

simple cameras made to use them, but are seldom used in serious photography.

Instead of flashbulbs you may want a strobe unit. This light will fire repeatedly with no changing of bulbs. It is powered either by batteries or by current from an electrical outlet. Strobe outfits are now available in small, cigarette-pack sizes and at modest prices. One advantage of strobe light is that it is suitable, without filtering, for either color or black-and-white film.

Beginning photographers often expect too much from flash cubes or electronic flash units. The next time you attend a night baseball game notice how many flashbulbs go off in the top rows of seats. These people are too far away from the playing field to get good flash pictures of the players. The best pictures you can make with a flash unit are at distances between six and fifteen feet from the subject. If you are closer than this you may overexpose, and from beyond twenty feet you might as well save your flash, because the light is unlikely to carry far enough to help.

If you want to cut down the light from a flashbulb for portraits and other close-up subjects, try covering the light with a single thickness of a cotton handkerchief. This will take a little practice before you know how much to expect of your light and your chosen film at a given distance.

Using a strobe unit, you may make the mistake of shooting the instant the little ready light flashes. It is true that the ready light tells you when the batteries have recharged the capacitors. But sometimes, after the first shot, it flashes too early, and if you fire the unit you get less light than you need for a good picture. The full length of time needed for recharging the capacitors may vary from one unit to the next, and you will have to learn how long your unit takes for a full charge.

You can do this with the help of a small AM transistor radio. Fire the light unit, then hold it against the radio, which is turned on but dialed where there is no station. As the capacitors recharge, you will hear static; when the static disappears, the capacitors are fully charged and ready to give full light for the next exposure. Note the time needed for this recharging. Then in future shots allow that amount of time instead of firing as soon as the ready light flashes.

Flash and strobe units ordinarily have their greatest use indoors where there is not sufficient light for good pictures without some supplemental light. But photographers also use flash outdoors to help fill in deep shadows on a face or other subject.

Most beginning photographers aim the flash unit straight at the subject; and when they do this shooting indoors, it is oftentimes a mistake. Straight-on flash, especially at close range, can remove all shadows, and the result is a flat light. In addition, the harsh frontal light

A flash used on the camera, while giving fewer problems in shooting action photos, often results in flat lighting and distracting shadows. (*Vivitar Corporation Photo*)

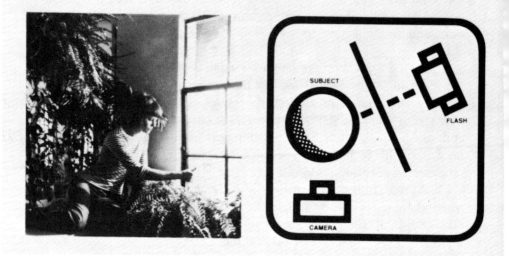

By placing the flash on the other side of the window, the picture appears more natural. (*Vivitar Corporation Photo*)

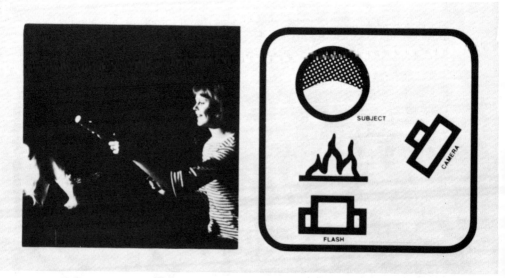

The subject appears to be illuminated by the fire because the flash is positioned outside the camera's view. (*Vivitar Corporation Photo*)

When using a flash to fill in deep shadows, expose for the existing light and limit the artificial light to a slight underexposure of the shaded areas by moving the light farther from the subject or attaching a neutral-density filter. (*Vivitar Corporation Photo*)

Under an overcast sky, this picture was given the appearance of being in sunlight by exposing for the flash instead of existing light. The flash is moved close enough to the subject to make it stronger than existing light. (*Vivitar Corporation Photo*)

 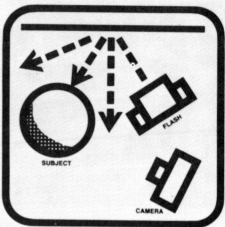

Indirect flash calls for pointing the flash unit away from the subject and bouncing the light off a white ceiling or wall to give a natural diffused light. (*Vivitar Corporation Photo*)

 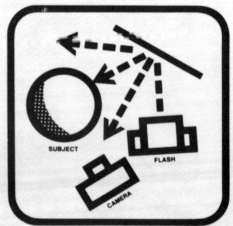

Outside, on an overcast day, indirect flash can be utilized by bouncing the light off a white reflector. Remember that the distance from flash to subject is the total distance from flash to reflector to subject. (*Vivitar Corporation Photo*)

 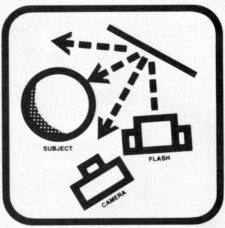

The glare from shiny surfaces can be cut down by bouncing light off reflectors. Because flash guide numbers are not useful where the size of the flash lens is larger than the area photographed, photographers making extreme close-up pictures depend on a trial-and-error procedure to determine the correct exposures. (*Vivitar Corporation Photo*)

can cast background shadows against walls, detracting from the picture. Heavy shadows are most troublesome when the flash unit is held close to the camera. This is one disadvantage of having a flash unit that is attached directly to the camera or the hot shoe. It is better to have a unit that is connected to the camera by a cord. This gives you freedom to hold the flash away from the camera.

Hold the flash unit as high as you can and slightly to one side; you will be surprised at how the shadows disappear and the subject takes on form.

If you use a flash unit connected to the camera by a cord, it is a good practice to carry an extra cord. The fine wires inside these cords have a tendency to break, often at the worst possible times.

For some pictures it is better not to point the flash toward the subject at all. Instead, let the light bounce off a nearby surface so it reflects back onto your subject. This is called "bounced" light. It should be used more often than it is, by beginners as well as old hands. Usually the flash is pointed toward a wall or the ceiling at an angle that bounces it back to the subject. Outdoors it can be bounced

Bounced light is an excellent technique for making indoor portraits with a soft light that eliminates harsh shadows. The light from the flash is aimed at a reflecting surface, not directly at the subject, and the exposure is adjusted accordingly. (*Photo by the author*)

off a reflector held so as to direct the light toward the subject.

Bounced light is superior for many subjects, even if you have to set up a tripod. If you are photographing a subject that will not move, you have plenty of time to use a tripod and move the light around any way you like. Even if you are shooting a portrait, you can do it in this manner. Your subject can hold still briefly if you have to use a longer exposure time.

One way to expose for bounced light indoors, with black-and-white film, is to take a meter reading of the available light. Set your camera for this light, then use an added light bounced from ceiling or wall to brighten the scene. Another rule, followed by some photographers, is to open the camera two stops over what the setting should be for direct flash. Experiment with bounced light until you find what exposures work best for you.

Some flash units are equipped with light sensors that automatically control the amount of light reaching the film. With this kind of unit you must know the distance from the subject to the light in order to set the sensor. But bounced light travels from the flash to the bouncing surface, and from there to the subject. This total distance is what you must measure or estimate.

9. SETTING YOUR CAMERA

TO MAKE THE BEST PICTURE, you must let exactly the right amount of light reach the film. The instant the camera is open, the light enters the camera, strikes the film, and records the image. Some film is more sensitive to light than others, and the camera must be set to take into account both the film speed and the amount and kind of light.

When you set the camera to make a picture, you have some leeway. With black-and-white film you can either underexpose or overexpose as much as two stops and still get a satisfactory negative. With color film, if you miss by more than half a stop in either direction, you will end up with an unsatisfactory picture.

You can tell by looking at the slide, or the black-and-white negative, whether or not your exposure was right. With color slides the overexposed pictures received too much light and are paler than they should be. Colors look washed out. If color slides are too dark, they were underexposed. But with black-and-white negatives it is the opposite. Overexposed negatives are too dark, while underexposed negatives are too light.

To adjust the camera for the light, you can change either the diaphragm or the shutter speed, or both. The first step, however, is to learn what the right exposure should be for the picture you want to make. Film speed, plus the diaphragm opening, plus the shutter speed, are what you need to consider in setting the camera.

MEASURING LIGHT

Even though you may have a camera that adjusts itself automatically, it is a good idea to learn how to use exposure meters.

The exposure meters built into many modern cameras are generally reliable. Some photographers also carry an additional exposure meter. The separate meter makes it easier to take readings when using a tripod. You may want to move in for a close reading off the subject without moving your camera. It also serves as a backup if the meter in the camera is not working properly.

The most common way to get a meter reading is to hold the meter so it averages out the light reflected from the various surfaces toward which it is pointed. But even then the meter can give you false information.

When using any exposure meter, remember that there is a human element in the process. Light meters should not only be read, but their readings must also be interpreted. The light meter picks up light

A young cook on a camping trip is worth a picture. By exposing for the shadows, the photographer was able to bring out the detail in the print during a darkroom session. (*Photo by the author*)

from all the surfaces in front of it, not just the part of the picture that is of special interest to you. Look at the areas around your main subject. If you are taking a picture of a girl but getting part of the light reading from a very dark background, the image of the girl may be overexposed. The light meter told you to open up the camera another stop or two and expose for the background. Another common mistake is to point the meter to take in too much light from the sky.

In this situation you should move in for a close-up light reading of the girl's face or dress. Professional photographers often carry a neutral gray card from which they take meter readings. This card, which you can get at a photography store, is held a foot or so in front of the meter to give you a reading of the average light at the time.

Sometimes it is hard to believe what the light meter says. Your best bet is to trust it anyhow. But you can also "bracket" your exposure. This means shooting the picture at the exposure you decide is correct, then shooting two more pictures—one after setting the lens for one stop more light, and another setting for one stop less. Professional photographers often bracket their exposures.

Here is a way to always remember the correct exposure for outdoor pictures in full sunlight. Set the camera at $f/16$ and the shutter speed at the ASA rating for the film you are using. If you are shooting a film rated at ASA 25, the setting would be $f/16$ and $1/25$ second, or the equivalent of this—for example $f/11$ at $1/50$ second, $f/8$ at $1/100$ second.

Another way, if you have no exposure meter, is to keep the slip of paper that is packed with each roll of film. Study that sheet. Among other things, it tells you the proper exposures for that film under various light conditions. These are sound directions and can be trusted. But remember that there is still a human element in the process. Your idea of an overcast sky, for example, may not be exactly what is described on the fact sheet. Or the subject of your picture may have an unusually dark background or highlights that could affect the exposure. If in doubt, the old practice of bracketing your exposures and shooting extra pictures is sound, especially if the picture is one you want very much.

The black-and-white negative should show detail in both the highlight and shadow areas. If the highlights are flat, it is overexposed. If the shadows show no detail, it is underexposed. Although no darkroom magic can bring out details that are not in the negative, a slight overexposure or underexposure can be corrected when making prints. Color slides, however, cannot be corrected.

As you take more pictures, you will become a better judge of light. You will be able to guess the right exposures for black-and-white film in good light. But when light is poor, or when shooting color pictures, you will need to check exposures carefully before setting your camera. Taking a meter reading is never a waste of time.

There is still the question of selecting the best combination of shutter speed and diaphragm opening for the picture. Several factors can figure into this. First, consider the shutter speed. If you are shooting action—for example, a football game—you will need to use a fast shutter speed. Otherwise your subject will be blurred. Fast action should be shot at speeds of at least 1/500 second.

Wildlife shots must often be made at fast speeds to avoid blurred images. (*Photo by the author*)

A shot of people walking may be blurred if you shoot as slowly as 1/125 second. Higher shutter speeds cut down the chances of blurred images.

But every time you increase shutter speed, you cut down the amount of light striking the film. This means you have to make up for the faster speeds by opening the diaphragm to a lower-numbered *f*/stop. If you increase the shutter speed by one stop, you must open the diaphragm one stop to allow the same amount of light to reach the film. For example, if the exposure were *f*/11 at 1/125 second, and you wanted to increase the shutter speed to 1/250 second (which is twice as fast as 1/125 second), you would have to open the diaphragm one stop to *f*/8.

But as you open the diaphragm, you reduce the depth of field. Depth of field is the area of the subject between the camera and infinity which is in sharp focus. The more you close the diaphragm down toward those higher-numbered *f*/stops, the deeper the area in front of the camera that is in sharp focus. What you have to do is reach a compromise between depth of field and shutter speed. Depth of field is usually satisfactory at medium distances when the camera is set at *f*/8 or higher.

In some pictures, great depth of field may not be important. If you are shooting an outdoor portrait, having the background slightly out of focus can actually improve the picture by blurring areas that might compete with the main subject for attention.

With medium-distance shots, most of the field can be kept in focus by focusing one third of the way into the picture. Some cameras have special buttons which, when pushed, stop down the diaphragm to the *f*/stop setting to show the areas that are in sharp focus. Some cameras also have a scale on the lens barrel that shows the area of the field in focus at any setting.

If subject movement is not a problem, and you want great depth of field—as you might, for example, in a landscape or a close-up of a flower—you can stop down the diaphragm opening to *f*/16 or *f*/22. But this may mean slowing down the shutter speed so much that you cannot safely hand-hold the camera. You may, for example (especially if the light is poor), have to shoot at 1/15 second or even 1/2 second. If so, use a tripod to avoid camera movement.

The closer your subject, the shallower the field in focus. If you are photographing distant subjects, such as a landscape, everything be-

Good photographers learn to be alert for fresh picture possibilities. Here the photographer waited until the canoes formed a pleasing pattern. (*Photo by the author*)

Care with depth of focus permitted the photographer to get all the important elements of this dramatic trout-fishing picture in focus on Snowmass Creek in Colorado. (*Colorado Department of Public Relations Photo*)

yond a certain point will be in focus. Depending on your lens, this may include everything from, say, twenty feet to infinity. When photographing subjects very close up, however, the depth of field may be only a few inches, or even a fraction of an inch. A grasshopper shot head-on may have its head in sharp focus and its tail out of focus. If the grasshopper stands still, you can correct this by making a longer exposure at a slower shutter speed, stopping down the diaphragm to gain greater depth. Or you can use artificial lights, which will enable you to shoot faster. You might also move to a side view of the insect, where you do not need as much depth to have all of the insect in focus.

Many modern cameras are equipped to do the photographer's thinking. They adjust automatically to give the exact exposure needed for the light available. Even if this is true for your camera, you should still learn how to set a camera manually. This is basic knowledge every serious photographer should have. You may not always have an automated camera available when you want to take a picture. Many automated cameras can also be set manually.

LEFT: When subjects are moving, try prefocusing on a spot ahead of them, then shooting as they reach that location. (*Photo by the author*)

OPPOSITE PAGE: Action photos, in which the subject is moving directly across the scene, should be shot at the fastest possible speed. (*Photo by the author*)

10. WAYS TO IMPROVE
YOUR PICTURES

WE ARE NOT ALL TRYING TO CREATE A WORK OF ART every time we push a shutter. Most of us take pictures the easiest way we know how. We are satisfied if the result is a likeness of friends, or a reminder of a pleasant trip. There is nothing wrong with this easygoing style of picture-taking.

But if you want your pictures to rise above the millions of average shots made every year, you are going to have to put more of yourself into the process of picture-taking. This means thinking about pictures. You begin to elevate your pictures to a new level when you start asking yourself, each time you pick up your camera: "How can I make this picture a little different and a little better?"

One way to train yourself for this is to study pictures other photographers have made. Professionals study each other's work.

When you thumb through a high-quality magazine that obviously employs top-ranking photographers, study the pictures. Try to figure out what length lens was used, how the picture was lighted, and why the photographer took it at the time of day he did, or under the special conditions he employed. What about the composition? Did the photographer succeed in what he or she tried to do?

The more you study pictures, the better you are able to "read" them. Discuss them with your friends and see which ones you think are outstanding, and why. For photographers this is fun and educational.

For photographing this family scene at the beach, the photographer chose a high angle and strong sidelighting to add emphasis. (*Michigan Department of Natural Resources Photo*)

CAMERA MOVEMENT

Beginning photographers sometimes do not understand how still the camera must be held. If you move the camera while shooting, even a little bit, you will blur the picture. This probably ruins more pictures than any other problem.

You can tell by looking at a picture if the camera moved. If the subject moved and the camera was held steady, only the subject will be blurred while the rest of the picture around it is sharp. But if the camera moved, every part of the picture will be blurred. It may not seem to be badly blurred when you are looking at the negative or a contact print, but when enlarged, the blurring is magnified and easily seen. Before making a print, photographers look at negatives under a magnifying glass to see if the image is sharp.

One way to keep from ruining so many pictures by camera movement is to learn the right way to hold a camera. Small cameras, including the 35mm models, should be firmly supported with one hand beneath them. The elbow of the arm holding the camera can be braced against the side of the body. The other hand can also help to steady the camera while one finger remains free to press the shutter release.

Do not snap the shutter release. Press it slowly and steadily. And in the brief instant you are actually shooting the picture, hold your breath. If you practice holding your breath at the moment you take the picture, and do this every time, you will soon find that you do it without thinking about it.

For most outdoor pictures you can hand-hold the camera and keep it steady. This is easy enough at shutter speeds of 1/125 second or faster. With great care, some photographers can shoot at speeds of 1/60 second, or even slower, and come up with sharp pictures. But the slower the shutter speeds, the greater the chance the camera motion will ruin the picture.

There are various aids, other than a tripod, you can use to keep the camera from moving when shooting at slow speeds. One is to brace it against a tree or building. Or you might rest the camera on a rock. If you use any part of an automobile for support, be sure the engine is turned off. Otherwise, vibration will jar the camera.

If you want to shoot a picture from a traveling car or an airplane, shoot at the fastest speed you can for the light you have available.

Hold the camera steady. The blurred picture was shot when the camera was moving. The other picture was shot when the camera was motionless. (*Photos by the author*)

And do not brace the camera against the window or any other part of the moving vehicle, where it will pick up vibration. Instead, brace it with your hands and head and try to pick a moment when there seems to be little jiggling or bumping in the vehicle.

Getting a good shot from a moving car is not easy, and you should expect to fail at it much of the time. Shutter speeds should be at least 1/250 second. It is easier to shoot an acceptable picture from an airplane than from an automobile. In either case, shoot at the fastest speed possible.

It is best to use some kind of support with any telephoto lens. A tripod is suitable if the subject is not moving. But if you are taking wildlife pictures, you may have to move with the subject. Instead of a tripod, you may place the telephoto lens on a shoulder brace, which you can buy from a photography store. Some photographers use gunstock mounts, either purchased or made by cutting a gunstock-shaped

By backing away from the tent and the people, the photographer included enough in the picture to show the setting and the rough weather that were part of the experience. (*Photo by the author*)

section from a piece of heavy wood. If you make your own gunstock mount, make it to fit your body. It will resemble the part of a rifle or shotgun that is made of wood, and it has to be equipped with a bolt to fit the tripod bushing on your camera.

Another aid in steadying a camera fitted with a telephoto lens is a monopod. It is a support with a single leg, a metal pole on which the camera rests while you are shooting.

Another lesson you can learn from expert riflemen is to use a sandbag under your camera. Get, or make, a small cloth sack. Pour dry sand into it until it is about three quarters full. You can also use dried beans. Placed on a hard surface, the bag provides excellent support for your camera.

If you must hand-hold your camera with a telephoto lens, remember to brace your elbows firmly against your sides, stand comfortably with your weight balanced on both feet, and hold your breath at the instant you press the shutter.

It is best not to shoot pictures at speeds of less than the focal length of the lens when hand-holding a long lens. With a 200mm lens, this rule would refer to shots at speeds slower than 1/200 second.

COMPOSITION AND MOOD

The person holding the camera has full control over what the picture will include. Point your camera slightly to one side or the other, or raise or lower it a fraction of an inch, and you have a different picture. If you study a few rules of good composition, you will begin to see improvement in the pictures you make.

Consider the arrangement of the subjects you see in the viewfinder. One basic rule says that the major point of interest should usually not be right in the center of the picture. The composition improves if the dog you are photographing, the running child, or the canoe, is a little to one side, and either above or below the center of the picture.

Most good pictures have a single point of interest which, by a movement of the camera, can be positioned where the photographer wants it. Think of your picture as divided into nine equal parts by two lines across it and two lines up and down, so that both the horizontal and the vertical are divided into thirds. This is known as the "rule of thirds." Then try to position the important element in your picture a

A common mistake of beginning photographers is cutting off the top of the subject's head. This is easily corrected by moving the camera. (*Photo by the author*)

third of the way to either side, and a third of the way from the bottom or top. If you are moving in for a tight shot and filling the viewfinder with a head-and-shoulders shot, or if you are shooting an arrangement of flowers, you may want the subject centered. But much of the time the rule of thirds can be followed.

In addition, try not to have subjects, especially moving ones, facing the edge of the picture they are closest to. Have them facing, running, or moving into the picture instead. Give them room for movement, so it does not seem to the viewer that they are running off the edge of the picture.

Do not include too much in a picture. Keep it simple and it is more likely to hold interest for the viewer.

Also, do not include a lot of foreground or sky in your pictures unless they help to tell a story or improve the composition.

Every object in a picture tends to draw the eye away. If there are

Pleasant composition and backlighting make this a successful picture. (*Photo by the author*)

objects in the picture that do not help tell the story you want to tell, exclude them if you can. For example, a bicycle lying in a front yard may detract from the picture of a house. Move the bike or photograph around it. The added trouble will pay off in a better picture.

Probably the greatest fault in composing pictures is that the photographer stands too far away from the subject. Move in on your subject and watch your pictures improve. Some professional photographers consider this the most important rule of all.

Study the lines in your composition, because there are ways to use them to express the mood you want the picture to convey. Gentle curving lines make pictures that are relaxing and cheerful. On the other hand, straight lines and sharp angles give the impression of

Try for pictures that tell a story. The subject here, with his metal detector and map, is obviously treasure hunting. (*Photo by the author*)

solid strength. Straight lines such as streets, railroad tracks, or fences should not run across a picture parallel to any of its edges. Instead, angle them across the picture as you compose it in the viewfinder.

Watch for pictures that capture a feeling or emotion.

The person photographed may be ecstatic over a football victory, depressed over the loss of a pet, or bored with a public speaker. Capture these moods and you make pictures that convey a story. Pictures are always more successful when the event is real. Simply asking a friend to "look sad" usually makes a sorry picture.

A large percentage of the photographs many of us make are of outdoor scenes. Try to get mood into these pictures too. For example, a boat harbor, with all the boats at anchor, and the reflection of blue sky and white puffy clouds on the motionless water can be a moody, sleepy scene. A thunderstorm sweeping across a wheatfield can create an entirely different mood.

Whatever the subject, search for an opportunity to get a little extra into it and give it a special emotion or mood. Such opportunities are worth watching for. Successful photographers know that when such events present themselves, the opportunity has to be grasped before the picture possibility vanishes. One photographer traveled to Mount McKinley National Park to make color pictures of the towering peak reflected in the calm waters of Wonder Lake. For days the mountain was hidden behind heavy clouds. Then miraculously it came into view. The photographer worked fast and captured the image of the snowy peak as it was reflected in the lake. It was well that he hurried. Minutes later, wind riffled the lake's surface, erasing the reflection, then clouds moved in to hide the mountain, and he never saw the peak again.

SHOOTING ACTION PICTURES

We have all seen it happen, and probably each of us has done the same thing time and again. We get ready to shoot a picture, then say, "OK, hold it!"

That stops all the action in midair. People at work stop working. Actors on the stage freeze. People having conversations stop talking and stare at the camera. What we get is a picture that looks stilted. In short, it says the photographer yelled, "OK, hold it!"

Composing the picture so that part of a tree is in the foreground adds depth to this cross-country skiing scene. (*Canadian Government Office of Tourism Photo*)

Good photographers learn how to stop action with their cameras, not their words. They want their pictures to show exactly what was going on. This kind of action photography is not important in most portrait work or in landscapes. But it is essential if you want to capture the action of a basketball or football game; the activities in a factory, store, or classroom; or the flavor of a conversation between a grandfather and grandson. For better pictures you need to stop the action without stopping the activity.

This can be done. Your camera does not even need a superspeed lens to stop some action. Often it is a matter of the photographer watching for the action to reach a peak and pausing there for an instant. The pause may be brief, but for the photographer who knows his or her business, it can be long enough to take the picture. Such pauses, when action peaks out, can be seen in the movement of the trombone player's hand, the hitting of a baseball, the rise of a pole vaulter.

The direction of travel in relation to the lens can make a difference. If the movement is directly across the scene, the motion may be more difficult to stop than when it is quartering toward or away from the lens.

If you specialize in shooting outdoor action, you will need a fast shutter speed. A speed of 1/25 second is going to give you too many blurred pictures. People moving around should be shot at speeds of at least 1/250 second. If the subjects are running, swimming, or jumping, use at least 1/500 second, and if you have it, 1/1000 second. Remember that each time you step up the speed of the shutter one stop, you must compensate by opening the diaphragm one stop to allow an equal amount of light to reach the film.

Also, if much of your shooting is of sporting events, or other fast-moving action, you will want to use a fast-speed film. It is possible to shoot film at faster-than-normal speeds, then overdevelop to compensate for the faster exposure. For example, Eastman Tri-X (rated at ASA 400) can be exposed as if it were rated at ASA 800, or faster, and developed for the higher speeds. But remember to shoot the entire roll at the same rating, or part of it will be developed incorrectly.

When shooting at faster speeds, however, you can expect to sacrifice some quality in your negatives because you lose some of the shadow details. This trade-off, however, may be an improvement, since the details in the shadow areas may be distracting in sports shots.

But if you shoot a subject that shows high contrast between the light and dark areas, it is a good plan to shoot at less than the indicated ASA rating, then make up for the added exposure by reducing the development time. Such overexposing and underdeveloping will bring out better detail in the shadows. This follows an old rule among photographers—"Expose for the shadows and develop for the highlights"—which is still an excellent plan.

A technique often used by professionals in shooting fast-moving subjects is to *pan* with the movement. Assume that the subject you want to photograph is a racing car. You focus on where the car will be, then point at the car and follow its progress in your viewfinder. Try to move the camera at the same rate as the car, and when it approaches the point where you want to photograph it, press the shutter without stopping the camera's motion. If done correctly, this movement will blur everything but the moving car. The blurred background even helps by emphasizing the speed of the car.

To stop action in indoor pictures, or outdoor night photos, it is best to use an electronic strobe unit as the main source of light. While the shutter is open the strobe fires very fast. The flash of light can peak so quickly that action is frozen, giving a sharp picture. Some nature photographers have learned to use strobe lights to stop the wing movement of flying birds so successfully that every feather shows.

The photographer who is shooting action pictures always has a better chance if he knows something about the subject. Although it is important to learn how to use your photographic equipment, it can be just as important to learn the rules of the game you are photographing. If you know what to expect, you will be ready not just for the expected but also for the unusual.

SHOOT A SERIES

Often it is best to think of pictures as a series of related shots. If you are taking a trip, you may want a slide show that tells the story of the adventure from beginning to end.

Or you may want a set of pictures showing how a club worked to clean up a local stream. Another time you may want to photograph the steps involved in tying a trout fly or caring for a house plant.

This is the kind of series shots that photojournalists often work out. The series tells a story in logical sequence, and it has an important place in albums and photo shows as well as in magazines and newspapers.

Each picture in a series should contribute to the series. If the story can be told in three pictures, do not use five. The pictures should look as if they belong together. In short series of a few pictures, this is done by trying for similar lighting, exposure, and background.

Try shooting a series to tell a story. These three pictures of a boy building a birdhouse give the viewer an idea of the steps in the process. (*Photos by the author*)

If you are going to shoot a series, start by writing down a list of the pictures needed. This shooting script tells you when the set is completed.

Too many camera owners are unhappy with their pictures. Sometimes they know what is wrong. At other times they just have a "feeling" that the picture is not quite right. The following list brings together the reasons for most of the bad pictures cranked out every year. They are faults anyone can correct. The result will be better pictures and greater confidence in your skill.

1. **Photographer stood too far away from subject.**
2. **Camera was not held level; people, trees, and buildings lean to one side.**
3. **Photographer chopped off friend's head.**
4. **Photographer held finger in front of lens.**
5. **Camera jiggled.**
6. **People photographed are not relaxed and natural.**
7. **Poor composition: too much in the picture; confusing backgrounds; utility poles growing out of heads, etc.**
8. **Picture underexposed or overexposed.**

11. PHOTOGRAPH
YOUR FRIENDS

YOU MAY ENJOY TAKING PICTURES of your friends. But have you noticed that some friends do not praise your pictures of them quite as much as you think they should? When you look at the pictures you may see the pleasant composition, soft lighting, and probably the good printing job. But the friend wants to be able to say, "It is a good picture of me."

If the photo strikes the subject as unflattering, don't jump to the conclusion that your friends do not appreciate good photography when they see it. Instead, give the picture some more thought. There is a good chance it could have been improved.

If you are making outdoor portraits, remember not to pose the subject looking directly into the sun. There are several reasons. If the sun is high, it may cast harsh shadows that mask out detail. If the sun is low, the light will illuminate the face evenly and flatten it out because of the lack of shadows. Also, the sun will make the person squint, instead of looking relaxed and natural.

Try to get soft lighting on the face to give the features depth and roundness. To do this, place your subject in subdued light, perhaps the shade of a tree. Even if the sun is out full and clear, the foliage may allow shafts of sunlight through, and this would not help the picture. Instead, you need light that is spread out, diffused, the way it would be if there were thin, high clouds.

Portrait photographers, working outdoors, often carry reflectors to cast extra light on the subject. The reflector can be moved around

Instead of lining up your friends in front of the camera, catch them in relaxed situations for better pictures. (*Photo by the author*)

until the subject is lighted the way you want. Several kinds of reflectors are used. One emergency reflector that works is a Space Blanket of the kind carried by wilderness campers. One side is aluminum-colored and can be manipulated to reflect light where you want it. Photographers also make reflectors by gluing sheets of aluminum foil to wood or cardboard. Even a white tablecloth, sheet, or piece of cardboard will throw some soft light onto the subject. This subdued

A grandfather repairing a fishing rod for a child makes an interesting human-interest shot. Fill-in flash was used to bring out detail in the faces. (*Photo by the author*)

light is better in portraits than the harsh light you get from a flashgun pointed directly at the subject. If you do use a flash to give added light, try bouncing it off some nearby light-colored surface to get a softer, natural-looking reflected light.

The best height for the camera in most portraits is the eye level of the subject. The resulting pictures have less distortion. You may also want to try other camera angles. But remember that high camera an-

Framing subjects can add depth to the picture. (*Photo by the author*)

gles and low camera angles emphasize certain parts of the face. A high angle is likely to make the nose look big and the chin small, while a low angle (looking up at the person's face) lengthens the neck and shortens the nose. This is why the straight-on shot is usually best—at least until the photographer knows from experience the effects to be expected from various camera angles.

Another rule that experienced portrait photographers follow is to stand several feet away from the subject. Moving in close emphasizes the nose and makes the hands (which are closer to the camera than the face) look large also. Even if you want a picture of only the head and shoulders, it is still better not to move in for a "tight" shot. Close-ups tend to show freckles and pimples in embarrassing detail, which the subject will hardly appreciate. The combination of soft light and reasonable distance can help avoid this. For this reason, some portrait photographers use a short telephoto lens.

There are also tricks that make heavy people and skinny people look better in pictures. If your friend is overweight, do not shoot from a straight-on front view. Have the subject turn slightly to one side. On the other hand, a thin person can often be made to look less skinny if photographed from the front instead of the side.

Bad backgrounds ruin many pictures of people. A good general rule is that the background must not distract from the subject. In most pictures of people you will want to keep everything out of the picture that is irrelevant to the subject. Fences, streets, automobiles, close-up foliage, other people, and buildings all tend to distract from the subject instead of adding to the picture. Move the person around until these objects can be eliminated. The best background of all is usually a plain sky. Where background problems cannot be eliminated, shoot at f/stops below $f/8$ to get less depth of focus and throw background subjects out of sharp focus.

Shoot more than one picture of your friend. The first one will probably be taken before the subject is relaxed.

PHOTOGRAPHING SMALL CHILDREN

Taking good pictures of small children takes patience, skill, and a dash of luck. But most photographers can improve these pictures if they remember a few guiding ideas.

The best time to photograph children is when they are having fun, as this boy on a visit to a national park. (*Photo by the author*)

Children are among the most photographed of all subjects. The best pictures catch them relaxed and happy. (*Clarence W. Koch Photo*)

The best pictures of children, as with older people too, are usually made when the subject is busy. He or she may be running in the sand, playing with a toy, or listening to a story. Pictures snapped at these moments are likely to have stronger appeal. Too often, straight portrait shots reveal the child's boredom with the whole procedure.

Giving the child directions—"Turn this way" or "Hold up the doll" —seldom creates the natural feeling you are after.

Pictures of children are best made at the child's eye level. This perspective invites the viewer into the child's world.

Backgrounds can be especially troublesome and distracting. You can block out some of them by throwing them out of focus. Use a setting of $f/5.6$ or $f/4$ to fuzz out the background.

You are likely to get better pictures also if there are not too many people around to distract you and the subject.

Children at play or work make excellent subjects. (*Photo by the author*)

12. TRY INDOOR AND CLOSE-UP PHOTOGRAPHY

EVEN IF YOU THINK YOU ARE A BASIC OUTDOOR TYPE interested mostly in photographing powerboats and mountain climbers, you can learn some important lessons by making pictures indoors with controlled lighting. You will not need a fancy studio setup. Neither will you need much room.

Besides, you can work on indoor pictures at night or when the weather is bad.

All you really need for a beginning is a table on which you can set up the objects you plan to photograph, and a couple of lights. The black-and-white film lights can be regular electric bulbs. Two bulbs will do for a start. One should be more powerful than the other—for example, a 100-watt bulb and a 60-watt bulb.

A basic arrangement is to place the large bulb at a position 45 degrees from the camera and shining on the subject. The smaller bulb can be placed at the camera. The camera should be on a tripod.

Then set up your subject. It might be vases, boxes, bowls, or arrangements of fruit or flowers. Avoid busy backgrounds, especially patterned wallpaper or curtains.

The advantage of this kind of arrangement is that it gives you a second chance if you do not like the way the picture turns out. You have time to make your picture, study it, then go back and shoot it again with different lighting. You may want to add a third light.

In this way you will begin to see how changing the lighting can improve pictures. These lessons in lighting can then be used in later shots, even when taking pictures outdoors. Outdoors you may not be able to move the light source, but you can usually pick your camera location.

Besides, you may surprise yourself and create photographs under controlled indoor conditions that deserve to be framed and hung on a wall.

Most cameras will not make film images much larger than one tenth the size of the subject. This is as close as the lens will allow the camera to come and still have the subject in sharp focus.

But for many kinds of pictures this is not close enough. When photographing a postage stamp, old coin, or other small object, we want to move in close to get a bigger image. If your lens is not built so that

A good way to study the effects of lighting on a subject is to work with controlled light on still-life arrangements indoors. Lights can be moved and pictures can be retaken until the result pleases the photographer. (*Clarence W. Koch Photo*)

you can move in close to the subject, you can buy inexpensive equipment to adapt it for the job. One solution is a set of close-up lenses. These are sometimes known as portrait lenses. They allow you to move in closer, so that the object fills more of the frame of film and still keeps the subject in focus.

With some single-lens reflex cameras it is possible to use a bellows between the lens and camera body. A bellows allows you to take extremely close-up pictures. The same effect can be accomplished by using extension tubes between the camera and lens. Using either the bellows or extension tubes, you will have to increase exposure times. The increase is called the bellows factor. With portrait lenses, however, you can take pictures at the same exposures you would use without the close-up attachment.

Some cameras are better than others for close-up photography. Single-lens reflex cameras are suitable because no matter how you adjust the camera, you still see the picture as you will take it. On twin-lens cameras, or cameras with viewfinders that do not let you see through the lens, the lens and the viewfinder are generally not co-ordinated for very close distances.

Camera motion and depth of field can be problems in taking close-ups. A tripod or other support is advisable.

For shooting close-ups the diaphragm should be stopped down to at least $f/8$. This may mean using slow shutter speeds. But you can do this if you are working with a tripod and a subject that doesn't move. The smaller $f/$stop gives you greater depth of field.

Close-up photography is an exciting way to make unusual pictures. It is also an excellent skill to develop because it could prove valuable in many kinds of professions, including biology, medicine, and engineering.

13. MAKING COLOR PICTURES

For a long time after cameras were invented photographers could use them only for taking pictures in black-and-white. There is nothing wrong with making black-and-white pictures. Some photographers prefer to work all their lives in black-and-white. Famed landscape photographer Ansel Adams always did prefer black-and-white. But most photographers today want to make color pictures. The human eye sees the world in color. Therefore, color pictures do the best job of recording the scene as the eye sees it.

You have a choice of two ways to make color pictures. You may want to make slides, or you may prefer prints.

If you make color slides, your transparencies are positive images. This means you can project light through them and see the picture on a screen as it was seen by the camera. These positive transparencies are what most publishers use to reproduce color pictures in magazines and books.

If you want to keep color prints, you will probably use a film that is a negative when it is developed. These negatives can be enlarged into full-color prints.

But if you want to use your color slides both for projecting and making prints, this is also possible. You can send the transparencies to a commercial processor and order prints made from them. With some color films, you can develop and make prints in your own darkroom.

Either kind of color picture is excellent for viewing or showing to friends and relatives time and again. Whether you make slides or prints depends on your preference. But remember that to get the most pleasure from slides, you will need a viewer or projector that magnifies them. Slides can be stored in trays or boxes, or in carriers that fit the projector so they can be shown repeatedly without being taken out of boxes and arranged every time. Enlarged color prints are usually kept in albums or framed and hung on the wall.

If you have only one camera and switch back and forth from black-and-white to color film, you may have a problem remembering what kind of film is in the camera when you are ready to take a picture. Days, or even weeks, may have passed since you used the camera last. The answer is to mark your camera so you can tell which film is in it. Some cameras are equipped with settings that tell this, provided the photographer remembers to change the setting every time he loads the camera with a different kind of film. Even if you carry two cameras, you may have trouble remembering which is loaded with color, and which with black-and-white. This may seem to be a simple point, but it is the source of endless confusion for many photographers. For that reason, it is best to work out a system and stick to it. Attaching a small piece of colored tape to the back or top of the camera, or using plain tape on which you can write "color" or "b&w," solves the problem. Or tape the tab from the film box to the back of the camera.

Some color films must be processed by the manufacturers or licensed laboratories. For example, Kodachrome is sent to such laboratories for developing. These laboratories return 35mm, 126 cartridge, and bantam-sized film to you, neatly mounted in 2x2 slide holders ready for the projector. When sending color film to the processor, you can either take it to the photo shop or send it to the lab in mailing envelopes that you buy from the camera store.

If you want to develop your own color film, you must select one for which the chemicals are available. Developing color film must be done very carefully and according to the directions packed with the processing kit.

Many subjects make more striking color pictures if the sky is overcast than when there is full sunlight. Try making scenic landscapes early in the morning or late in the evening for rich, warm light. Also try backlighting some of your color pictures for added drama. On a bright day a backlighted subject may call for opening the camera up one or two stops over what the exposure would be with sun shining directly on the subject.

Remember that color film, because it is usually slower than black-and-white, may often require a tripod, especially if you are shooting in low light.

Until you understand your camera and film well, concentrate on subjects that are well lighted and colorful. Then, as your knowledge grows, exciting new picture possibilities will open for you.

14. RECORD YOUR TRIPS
ON FILM

LONG AFTER A SUMMER VACATION or winter ski trip, your pictures will bring back memories of those good times. Pack the camera, buy some extra film, and promise yourself enough time during your travels to take the best possible photographs you can.

The kind of pictures you take will depend on where you are going. If you are headed for Yellowstone or some other famous scenic area, you will want pictures that show what the region looks like, shots of Old Faithful, the Falls of the Lower Yellowstone, and some high-angle shots looking down on one of the famous rivers flowing through the park.

In addition, you will watch for the wild animals, which are excellent subjects. In Yellowstone you can add pictures of buffalo, elk, moose, bears, and other animals to your collection. Whenever possible, photograph them in settings that also help to tell the kind of country they live in. Not all of the national parks offer such excellent wildlife photographic possibilities. But each park has its own special features. The idea is to find what sets the area apart from others and capture those differences on film. In Acadia National Park in Maine, you may photograph the seashore. In Florida's Everglades there will be pictures of flat expanses of sawgrass and shots of alligators.

Wherever you vacation, you will want to take pictures showing what people do there for fun, and especially what you and the group you traveled with did. Perhaps it was fishing for trout in Yellowstone Lake. Show not only the fishing, but also back off enough to capture

The sand dunes and mountains of Death Valley make interesting patterns in the late-evening light. (*Photo by the author*)

This snapshot can be a remembrance of a favorite trip for the whole family. (*Photo by the author*)

Historic buildings make good subjects. In photographing this building, the birthplace of President Grant at Point Pleasant, Ohio, sidelighting was used to give depth and to highlight details. (*Photo by the author*)

something of the surroundings. Then move in for close-up shots of the fish and fisherman.

If you are camping, take pictures of your camp. You may also want a close-up picture of the sign at the park entrance, because this can be used as the introductory picture when you arrange a slide show of your trip. Wherever you travel, keep an eye open for the unusual. Try for pictures that are a little different from those made by all the other travelers.

The time to think about how you will take care of your camera while you travel is when you are getting ready for the trip. If you are going mountain climbing or horseback riding, for example, your camera could take a beating unless you take special precautions to protect it.

On a backpack trip do not settle for a few pictures of friends walking along the trail. If the camera is ready all the time, you can add a lot of variety to the picture record of your trip. There will be chances to photograph a friend digging food out of the pack for lunch, setting up a tent, climbing a tricky rock formation, or stopping for a close-up look at a wildflower beside the trail. These "unposed" action shots will enrich your picture collection.

Whether you are off on an outdoor-type vacation or a trip to a large city, you will find excellent subjects for good pictures. Keep the camera close by, use it, and work for variety in your pictures. It can add fun to the trip and make the memories last for years.

LANDSCAPE PICTURES

Most of us use our cameras now and then to take pictures of landscapes. Travelers often point their cameras at mountains, lakes, and forests. But too often these pictures are made casually. The vacationer steps out to the edge of a cliff overlooking the river, lifts camera to eye, snaps one quick shot, then turns and heads back to the car wearing a victory smile.

This kind of picture deserves more time and thought; good scenics are worth the effort needed to take them. Besides, most cameras can take better landscape pictures than they do. It is all up to the photographer. Some people have a better eye for a picture than others do. But almost anyone can improve his or her ability to "see" a good picture.

Rule one is to think before you shoot. The fact that the view is grand and full of beauty does not rule out the need to look at it carefully and think about the best way to photograph it. Use the viewfinder to help you compose the picture. What you are searching for is one feature that will be the main point of interest in the picture. It might be a mountain peak, a cliff, or a brook. If you could photograph everything you see spread out before you, you would have too

Anyone visiting Death Valley National Monument in California can take a picture like this one. The best times of day are early and late, when the low sun adds interest by contrasting highlights and shadows. (*Photo by the author*)

much in the picture to attract the eye to one special point of interest. Studying the scene framed in the viewfinder will help you to select the part of the scene that tells the story best.

This is the kind of picture you have time to do right. The mountain or lake is not going anywhere. If you want, you can set up a tripod. Or you can wait for the best light. If you come upon the big view at high noon, and the light is full on the scene, it may flatten out the features of the landscape. A cross-lighting or low light earlier or later in the day can give the scene depth, with shadows and highlights. The difference in the pictures can make waiting worthwhile.

Another point to consider in the lighting of a distant view is haze. Throughout much of the country the amount of haze has increased greatly in recent years because of air pollution. Skies are grayer than they once were. The haze seems always to be there in the distance. If you are shooting color film, the haze can give the scene a bluish cast because it reflects blue light from the sky. With any kind of film, filters are generally needed for landscape pictures. Haze filters or polarizing filters can be used with either color or black-and-white film. Yellow, orange, and red filters are useful with black-and-white pictures, depending on the circumstances.

When selecting the view to photograph, watch for moods in the landscape. Fog settling in a valley, mist over a lake, the clear rich colors of late evening can all add a special extra to your pictures.

Distant subjects often lose that feeling of depth you had when you saw it with your own eyes. Standing on the edge of the cliff, you sense the distance because you are part of the scene. But your camera does not see you in the scene. You can correct this by moving back a little and including something in the foreground. It may be only the edge of the cliff. Or it might be a tree. Photographers often have a companion in the foreground of such pictures. If you do this, don't have the person looking at the camera or even standing close to it, because the main point of interest then becomes the person, not the view. Instead, have the person also looking at the view, perhaps sitting comfortably on a rock. A person in the foreground may add depth and interest to a big scene, providing the figure does not become dominant.

But take a second shot also, this time without the person in the foreground. It is worth experimenting and worth the film. You may never be in this place again to retake the pictures you missed.

Another way to add depth to a view shot is to frame it in a fringe of foliage. The shape of the frame guides the eye naturally to the point of major interest.

Taking good pictures at the seashore can be difficult. The scene is broad and flat. Again the problem is finding a special point of interest. But it can be done. Possibilities include big waves washing in to shore, surfboarders,' boats, and birds. These accessories, however, can easily become the major point of interest. When this happens, your picture changes from a seascape to a picture of a bird, boat, or what-

This photograph demonstrates how adding people to a scene changes the emphasis of a picture. The choice depends on the photographer's purpose. (*Photo by the author*)

Historic sites, such as the North Bridge at Concord, Massachusetts, make excellent vacation-trip photo subjects. In this picture, the lines of the bridge lead the viewer's eye to the Minuteman statue on the other side. (*Photo by the author*)

ever. You must study the scene and move around until you are satisfied with the composition of your picture. You will find that you can arrange the scene to emphasize any part of it you want to. The choice is strictly up to you. But the picture will be a better one if you choose a single point of major interest.

Sunsets are tempting to photographers. The way to catch the

Bad weather can mean good pictures. Don't put your camera away just because the sun goes behind a cloud. Make the bad weather work for you and you will often capture dramatic and unusual pictures, such as this one of a small boat in fog. (*Photo by the author*)

beauty of a sunset is with color film. Try one shot slightly underexposed; another, a half stop overexposed. The difference can be dramatic. The underexposed one will probably be dark and dramatic; the overexposed one, soft and misty. When the orange sun is very close to the horizon, you can often take interesting pictures of figures silhouetted in front of it.

Black-and-white sunset shots can also be dramatic. The shape and density of the clouds are important, so this is a good time to try using filters. Also, take care to screen out direct sunlight from the lens. But if the sun begins to drop behind a dark cloud, watch the rays of light that fan out from it. This kind of scene can make a very dramatic picture.

Waterfalls always invite picture-taking. Few photographers can resist them. But the rapidly falling water is a challenge. The big question is, What shutter speed to use? If you shoot at too fast a speed, the water "freezes" in place and loses its natural appearance. But if you shoot at a speed too slow, the moving water becomes a blur. Choose a moderate speed—say, 1/125 second.

Another problem involves the light color of the water against the darkness of the nearby vegetation and rocks. If the sky is slightly overcast the contrast will not be so pronounced.

15. ANIMAL PICTURES

TAKING PICTURES OF ANIMALS IS FUN, but not always easy. Your subjects may not take directions well. They may even run away, leaving the photographer looking at an empty scene. But animal pictures are popular, so popular that some professionals make their living photographing nothing but animals. Some of these professionals work with pets, including dogs, cats, and horses, while others work only with the skittish wild creatures that live in forests and fields. For most of us, however, it is enough to get a good picture of the family pet or a vacation-trip shot of a deer or bear that wanders into the campground.

If you want to take outstanding pictures of your pet, try for something more than the usual snapshot. Study the animal. You already know better than anybody else what he does when he is at his funniest, or saddest, or when he is being especially impish. These are the traits by which he will be remembered. Try photographing the pet playing with another animal. If it's a kitten or puppy, snap him while he's playing with a favorite toy.

Let the camera see the animal from its own eye level. A low camera angle can give a whole new twist to your pet pictures. Some pet photographers accomplish this by posing the pet on a stand while taking the picture. If the animal will stay there, its mobility is limited and you can keep your subject in focus easier than if the pet were free to roam.

Many times, by working with him for a while, you can coax a dog into special attitudes or poses. Speak to him and see if he cocks his head sideways with that special inquisitive look he sometimes has. Try a squeaking sound that might be an imitation of a bird or mouse, and watch for the reaction. But be ready to shoot the picture the instant he does something interesting, because his moods can change rapidly and the opportunity is gone. Have the camera prefocused and adjusted for the right exposure so that all you have to do is frame the picture and shoot.

One rule for taking good pet pictures is to shoot a lot of film. You will probably not show all of the pictures to anyone, but you can sort out the very best, the really outstanding shots. Shoot the animal in different settings, at different times of the day, and work with him often. Begin to take pictures of the pet when it is only a puppy or kitten, because young animals have a special appeal. Keep at it and you stand an excellent chance of capturing some rare moments on film.

WILDLIFE PICTURES

If you move on to wildlife photography, you enter one of the most challenging of all hobbies and one that could even become a profession. Wild-animal photography is much more complex than taking pictures of your pets. The skittish white-tailed deer, the sharp-eyed turkey, or even the robin in the front yard prefer to be left alone. Their world is filled with threats, and they survive only if they are alert and ready to escape at the first sign of danger. The photographer who is stalking them is obviously not part of their wild community. For this reason, a wildlife photographer has to work out some tricky procedures to get close enough to his subjects to take good pictures.

First, consider your general behavior around wild animals. Most wild animals have keen senses developed over ages of evolution. Deer, for example, have two superior senses going for them. Their hearing is so keen that they can detect the rustling of leaves across a valley. They can identify human odor a quarter of a mile away if the person happens to be upwind. Either of these clues will be enough to send the deer slipping off through the woods, and the photographer will probably never realize how close he was to the animal.

Deer, on the other hand, may come very close if you make no un-

Close-up shots of wild animals, such as this bull elk, are best made with long lenses. Remember that wild animals can be dangerous. (*Photo by the author*)

natural noises, stay downwind, and do not move. You may even be out in the open and not be seen by a deer under these circumstances. Deer have poor eyesight, but they can detect sudden movement, and this is worth knowing. Wildlife photographers must understand such facts. The best wild-animal photographers are also first-rate naturalists.

Even birds, with their sharp eyes, may not pay much attention to a person who does not move. Movement is a dead giveaway. Test this yourself. Watch the treetops to see if there are birds there. You may see nothing. Then a bird, and it may be the smallest warbler, flits from one limb to another and you pick up the movement instantly. The wildlife photographer must either stay hidden, or stay so far from the subject that the animal acts naturally while it is photographed.

This is done in a couple of ways. One way is to use telephoto lenses, which reach out and bring the subject in close. Even without them you can take interesting wildlife pictures. But if you plan to do a fair amount of wildlife photography of large subjects, you will need a telephoto lens. If you use a 35mm camera, you should have a lens at least in the 200mm range.

Care, patience, and luck permitted the photographer in Yellowstone National Park to catch a mother elk and young in the same picture. (*Photo by the author*)

A roseate spoonbill is only one of the large wading birds that can, with luck and patience, be photographed on a visit to the Everglades National Park in Florida. Sidelighting adds interest, and the highlight in the eye adds sparkle to this wildlife shot. (*Photo by the author*)

A winter feeding station for birds can provide opportunities for pictures, such as this song sparrow taken through a window. (*Photo by the author*)

The other way to take close-up pictures of wild animals is to use a blind. A blind is anything that will hide you and your camera from the wild animal being photographed. Skilled photographers can sometimes move their blinds to within a few feet of a bird's nest, or close enough to a fox's den to make pictures of the pups playing in the sunshine at the entrance. Often a blind and a telephoto lens are both needed to get close-up images.

One of the most commonly used blinds is an automobile. In many places wild animals have become so accustomed to the presence of automobiles that they are not spooked when a car stops close by. As long as the photographer stays in the car, he can often take all the pictures he wants. This works especially well for large animals like deer, which are often found near the roads in state and national parks and in wildlife refuges. But step out of the car, and the deer will probably melt into the woods.

When photographing from a car, it is best to roll a window down far enough so that you are not shooting through the glass. Turn off the engine while you are shooting. This cuts down vibration, which can cause camera movement and result in blurred pictures. Some photographers who like to take pictures of ducks, geese, and swans watch for places where they can back their station wagon or pick-up close to the water. Then they hang a curtain of camouflage cloth in the back of the vehicle and shoot through slits in the curtain—all the while hidden from the nervous birds. In this kind of situation, especially when using a long lens, it is advisable to use a tripod.

If you become serious about wildlife photography you may want a portable photo blind. Lightweight canvas can be sewed into a little tent that drapes over a framework made of aluminum poles. Such a blind should have small windows in the sides for cameras, and a screened window near the top for ventilation on a hot day. The blind does not have to be high enough to stand up in, merely high enough so that you can sit on a low stool. But you'd better make yourself comfortable. You may have to stay in the blind for several hours to get the picture you want.

If the subjects saw you go into the blind but not come out, they sense that danger is still present. One trick that often works is to have a friend go into the blind with you, then leave after a few minutes, while you stay behind. Wild animals do not count well and will soon decide that all is well and settle back into their natural behavior patterns.

A single wild duck and its reflection make a simple but interesting shot when positioned off-center in the composition. (*Photo by the author*)

More important than whether or not you get the picture is the welfare of the wildlife you are photographing. Careless photographers can harm wildlife in various ways. One way is by chasing a parent bird away from the nest in order to get pictures of the young. A short time in the hot sun can kill young birds. Visiting a nest can also leave clues for predators who may follow you later and take the young. Touching a bird's nest, eggs, or young may cause the death of the young. Some wild parents will abandon their young if their nest is disturbed. It is far better to stay well back from any bird nest and use telephoto lenses. Birds that have just begun to build a nest, or have not sat on the eggs for long, will abandon their nest more quickly than those that are well into their nesting cycle. If you think there is a chance that your picture-taking may cause the nesting effort to fail, leave and look for another subject.

The photographer also has to think about his or her own safety. Some wild animals can injure people. Even birds will sometimes attack people to protect their nests or young. And if you should discover a mother bear, of any species, with young, make pictures only if you can do so from inside an automobile or building. Otherwise, get out of there.

This backlighted picture of a buffalo was made during a visit to Wind Cave National Park as the animal was sighted against the skyline. (*Photo by the author*)

Watch for the unusual. Wildlife photography is no different from photographing a school football game in this respect. You want to record the most memorable events. This may be the instant the deer stops eating to listen, or the moment when two male robins get into a heated battle over territorial rights. If you know how an animal acts most of the time. you will recognize the unusual at once and photograph it. Watch for chances to photograph such action as the feeding of young, taking of prey, courtship and breeding activity, or the play of young animals. Catch these moments and your wildlife pictures will rise above the ordinary.

Two examples come to mind. In Florida a professional wildlife photographer, hidden in his tree blind, saw a pine tree break off at the exact point where a pileated woodpecker had its nest. The woodpecker's eggs were exposed. Then, to the photographer's amazement, the parent birds picked up the eggs one at a time and flew off with them to a second nest they had already prepared in another tree.

Another photographer was on the scene when a green heron, which is a fish-eating bird, began to drop items into the shallow water. When fish rose for the bait, the heron snapped them up.

Neither of these amazing occurrences had ever before been known to happen. But both were photographed in color, and both appeared in the pages of *National Geographic*.

Some nature photographers specialize in pictures of insects or flowers. These call for special close-up attachments. They may also require as much patience as taking pictures of larger animals.

If you specialize in wildlife photography, you are starting a camera hobby that could last a lifetime. There is no end to the subjects. You may not see your pictures in the pages of a national magazine, but who can say?

16. PICTURES AT THE ZOO

THE NEXT TIME YOU GO TO THE ZOO, notice how many of the visitors are carrying cameras. Zoo visitors shoot millions of rolls of film every year. Their cameras are important because pictures help them to recall the exciting events of a special day.

But you may notice that many of their pictures are of friends standing in front of cages. There is nothing wrong with this if you want pictures of your friends in front of cages. But others who carry cameras to the zoo take advantage of the unusual opportunity to concentrate on the animals and their activities. As a result, they come home with pictures that are better than ordinary zoo snapshots. A zoo visit can become an exciting photo safari. You can photograph wild creatures from Africa, India, and other distant lands. These can be used in slide shows to present to clubs, in photo albums to show to friends, or for school projects.

Pictures taken at the zoo, however, can also be disappointing. Animals kept in cages behind bars are difficult to photograph. Often there is also a fence outside the cages to keep visitors from getting close enough for a bear or tiger to reach out and injure them with its claws. The best zoos for picture-making are the modern ones where the animals are kept out in the open, separated from the visitors only by moats or trenches. Some zoos and animal parks now let the animals roam freely and keep the people enclosed in rail cars or automobiles. You may see giraffes, lions, elephants, and ostriches, with no bars to separate animals and visitors. This is a big improvement.

An Andean condor photo-
graphed in the Cincinnati
Zoo. (*Photo by the author*)

Backgrounds for your pictures need no longer be cage walls.

In these open environments, however, the animals may be some distance away and you may need a telephoto lens to get good pictures. Other smaller and less dangerous animals will probably be close enough to photograph with a standard lens.

Special care is required if you must shoot through a fence, or through glass. Glass can present problems because of reflected light. Try shooting these pictures by holding the camera at an angle between 40 and 75 degrees to the glass surface. The glass may also reflect the glare of a flashgun, especially if the flash is pointed straight at the glass surface.

If you want to photograph fish in an aquarium, increase your exposure, even if the water looks absolutely clear. You may want to shoot more than one exposure so that later you can choose the best one to print or project.

Exposure meters can pick up reflected light from a glass surface and give false readings. Avoid this by holding the meter right up against the glass.

If you use a self-adjusting strobe unit, remember that it can be affected by its own light reflected from the glass surface. The safest procedure, where possible, is to take the picture with available light unless you have floodlights and understand their use.

If you have to shoot through wire cages, try to throw the wire out of focus. This can sometimes be done so that the wire is scarcely noticeable. Hold the camera close enough to the wire to keep the animal in focus and the wire out of focus. You may be able to position the lens between openings in the wire, provided you are not exposing yourself to danger from animals on the other side.

You still have the problem of catching the animal doing something interesting. Some zoo animals spend a lot of time sleeping. There may be little else for them to do, but this makes a dull picture. If you are patient you will probably have the opportunity to photograph the animals walking, stretching, drinking, eating, fighting, or yawning. The result will be a more interesting picture, worth waiting for.

If you have a choice of days when you can go to the zoo, choose one on which there are fewer visitors. On holidays and weekends many zoos are crowded. This can give the photographer extra problems as people walk in front of the camera or crowd the railings. The photographer, however, must remember that every visitor has an

Pictures such as this one of a family of Canada geese can often be made at zoos, city parks, and wildlife refuges. (*Photo by the author*)

equal right to watch the animals. Before school is out in the spring, and after it starts in the fall, are often good times to take a photo safari to the zoo.

Some zoos have special children's sections. These can be excellent places for photographers to work if they are allowed there. The animals are gentle and accustomed to having people close to them. In addition, children also make good subjects when they interact with animals.

Never become so wrapped up in your picture-taking that you forget that animals can be dangerous. Stay out of areas where visitors are not allowed. Feed only those animals that visitors are encouraged to feed. Many zoo animals have special diets which are essential to their good health. Some animals are worth thousands of dollars, or are so rare that they can not be easily replaced.

Remember that animals will defend themselves, especially if they become frightened. This reaction is natural. Harassing animals is never justifiable, and the desire for an interesting picture is no excuse.

Some zoo animals are photographers' favorites. The big animals, including elephants, giraffes, lions, and African antelopes, are always popular subjects.

Keep a pocket notebook with you at the zoo, and take notes on the animals you photograph. The signs on the cages will usually give their scientific names, country of origin, and other details. These facts add interest to any slide show, album, or school report in which the pictures are used.

You may have to make several trips to the zoo before you collect a satisfactory set of animal pictures. But every visit can add new trophies to your collection, fresh discoveries about animals, and effective ways to photograph them.

This picture of our national bird, the bald eagle, was taken at the Cincinnati Zoo. (*Photo by the author*)

17. WINTERTIME PHOTOGRAPHY

IN SUMMER WHEN THE SUN IS SHINING, picture-taking is easiest. But the photographer who stores his camera away on a shelf for those long winter months misses a lot. First, there are lessons to be learned by making pictures during the snowy season. And there are opportunities for making dramatic storytelling pictures that less adventuresome photographers are passing up.

Cold-weather photography brings some special problems. Winter snow scenes can make dramatic photographic subjects, or they can come off as dull and flat. The result depends on the light at the instant you shoot the picture. You need to think about both contrast and the intensity of the light. On a cloudy day the scene may be flat because there are no shadows to give it form. On the other hand, a brilliant sunny day may flood out the details in the highlighted areas.

For these reasons, choosing the best exposure for a snow picture is not always easy. Remember, you still have the help of your exposure meter, and the meter can come closer to giving the best exposure than any human guess. Instead of pointing the meter directly at the snow, point it at a neutral surface such as the back of your hand or a gray card.

You are likely to get snappier snow scene prints by underexposing black-and-white film by one stop, then overdeveloping it slightly to bring out detail in the light areas. This works best where there are no large shadow areas. It helps give texture to the snow.

Blue light is a problem for the photographer working in snow. In bright weather the blue light from the sky is intense. In addition, the snow is much bluer than we realize. Snow scenes are affected by ultra-violet rays, which are not detected by the human eye but are picked up by the film. Because of this abundant blue light, your black-and-white snow scenes may show less detail than you expect. The shadows become very light instead of showing texture. The answer is to use filters.

Action adds to outdoor pictures. Stopping fast-moving skiers calls for shutter speeds of at least 1/500 second. (*Canadian Government Office of Tourism Photo*)

When photographing snow scenes such as this ice fisherman, texture is often improved by a slight underexposure, then overdeveloping. (*Photo by the author*)

For black-and-white snow scenes, use an orange or yellow filter. Orange is generally better.

If you are shooting color, you should equip the lens with a skylight filter, even on an overcast day. This filter will help control the blue light and give you all-around better color rendering.

With either black-and-white or color film, a polarizing filter can help you to get snappy winter scenes. It gives form to details in the snow and intensifies the blue of the sky. If your camera is equipped with a built-in light meter, you will automatically get the proper exposure adjustment for any filters that cut down the amount of light admitted to the film. But if you are using a camera without a built-in meter, remember to make allowances for the filter in your exposure settings.

Snowy days are excellent times to try for unusual and dramatic shots. Don't stay indoors when the wind is drifting snow around fence posts and parked automobiles. Get out in the weather and try for dramatic pictures. Good photographers do not confine their efforts to making pictures they know will "come out." Instead, they push their equipment and test their skills. You will often find that the picture you thought hadn't a chance turns out to be the most exciting and dramatic one of the day.

Working in very cold weather requires some added care to keep cameras and films working the way you want them to. Most cameras today come from the factory ready to work in either winter or sum-

This picture of an ice fisherman on frozen Lake Erie captures the feeling of bitterly cold wind and the comfort of the fishing shanties. (*Photo by the author*)

mer. But on zero days the working parts of the camera may move sluggishly. Keep the camera under your coat when it is not in use. If the camera is cold and you take it into a warm area, the lens may fog up. Your warm breath on the lens or viewfinder will fog it up also. The camera store sells a lens-cleaning liquid that helps to prevent fogging.

Very cold weather can also sap the energy from batteries in a flash unit or in the light meter, and if you are going out for a long time, it is a good idea to carry extra batteries with you.

Film becomes brittle in very cold weather. Unless it is wound slowly and carefully, it can break. Brittle film is difficult to load without causing damage. This is another reason for keeping the camera under your coat when it is not in use. It can be given extra protection from flying snow by enclosing it in a plastic bag.

Then, when you go outdoors for skiing, hiking, skating, or ice fishing, take your camera along. You will probably add unusual pictures to your collection.

18. OUTFITTING
YOUR DARKROOM

ONCE YOU HAVE LOADED YOUR CAMERA with black-and-white film, pointed it at the subject, and pressed the shutter, you still have not made a picture. But you have made a beginning. The light that flowed through the lens to strike the film made changes in the coating of silver particles on the emulsion side of the film. But that image is invisible. It is a latent image. To make it visible, the film has to be run through a chemical process that develops the latent image. This developing process is not as complicated as it seems at first.

One immediate need is a completely dark area where you can open the roll of film for handling. If you were to open it where light could reach it, the silver coating on the film would come out black when developed. Even a little bit of light can make it cloudy and ruin the pictures.

But you do not need a fancy, expensive darkroom. Instead, you can use any part of the house where you can completely block out the light. Such a place is easiest to find at night. It might be the bathroom or even a closet. If you use developing tanks, which are light-tight, all you need is a dark area large enough to load the film on the tank's spool. With the tank loaded and closed, you can come out of the darkened room and perform the remaining steps of the developing process in full light. The sensitive film is safe inside the dark tank. If film is developed in trays, the room must be completely dark throughout the developing process.

When you think you have found a room dark enough to unwind the roll of film, sit there with the lights out for five minutes before opening the film. When you first go in and shut the doors and windows, the room may seem as black as a cave. But after a time your eyes begin to adjust and you can tell whether or not the room is truly dark. Often you will begin to notice a faint glow of light around the edge of the door, or a stray beam from a streetlight outside the window. Cover these cracks with folded towels or with black paper taped in place.

If there is no way you can find a darkroom, you may want to buy a changing bag at the photographic shop. This is a black, light-proof, zippered cloth sack with holes for your arms to fit through. It forms a snug fit around your wrists to block out light. Once it is shut, no light gets inside. Put the developing tank and the film into the dark bag, close it, and do not open it again until you have loaded the film into the developing tank and shut it tightly.

This way you can develop film without a darkroom, but you must still find a place to make prints. This also calls for a darkroom, because the printing paper is sensitive to light. It is less sensitive than film, however, and while printing you can use a dim light-amber "safe-light," which casts enough light to let you move around in the darkroom without stumbling over the wastebasket.

For printing you must use open trays of chemical solutions, and the darkroom has to have space for this equipment as well as a print box or enlarger, and boxes of paper, and cans and bottles of chemical solutions. You will also need a source of water, preferably running water. Printing and enlarging are often done in the kitchen, where there is running water. A laundry room in the basement might also work well, and the bathroom can become a temporary photographic darkroom.

Wherever you decide to work, check before you begin to see that you have space enough for everything you will need in the processing. You may need to set up a small table or a folding card table. Or you might, as some photographers do, give yourself added work space by covering the bathtub or laundry tubs with a sheet of plywood. Once you think everything is in working order in your new darkroom, it is always a good plan to run through the various processing steps using plain water, to be sure that you will not face an emergency at a critical moment unprepared. This test run can give you added confidence, and perhaps also save some pictures.

If you are going to build a new permanent darkroom, try to find an area that does not have to be used for anything else. A darkroom is not a good place for storing rugs, auto parts, canned goods, or anything else except the materials needed for developing and printing pictures.

Setting up a darkroom calls for ingenuity. Usually there are more possibilities than we see at first. Building and equipping a darkroom do not have to involve a major expense. If there is a small room in the basement where you can run water in easily, you have a head start. If not, you may want to wall off a corner and create such a room. You may block off a section of the basement by covering partitions with black tarpaper stapled or taped in place. Tarpaper can also be used for covering windows. Photographers have also shut out light by painting windows black or using black plastic. If there is no easy way to have running water in your work area, do not let this stop you. You can use plastic water buckets and carry water.

If you must use a part of the house where there are finished surfaces, cover them first with sheets of plastic or other materials that will protect them from the chemicals. If you should spill or splash chemicals where they might harm a surface, be quick to wipe them up.

A good idea for a photographer about to set up his or her first darkroom is to visit a more experienced photographer who has had a darkroom long enough to get the bugs out of the system. It will give tips and shortcuts, ideas that work, to save time and simplify darkroom jobs. Photographers like to share their findings. Darwin Bass is a professional photographer for the Cincinnati Gas and Electric Company. His job entails all kinds of assignments, from making a portrait of the company president to shooting aerial photographs of a new cooling tower at the nearby nuclear power plant. At work he uses his company darkroom. But, like many professionals, he does not stop thinking about photography when he comes home. He may be making pictures of his own, or working in the darkroom he has built in his own basement. "I do not think you have to spend a fortune to set up a darkroom," Bass says. "I go on the theory that, except perhaps for the enlarger, the equipment in a darkroom does not have to be fancy or expensive. People throw away items that could be put to work."

Step into his darkroom and you notice at once that the room is divided down the middle. There is a purpose for this: All the wet materials are kept on one side of the darkroom, and all the dry materials on the other. "This is ideal," says Bass, "but for some people it isn't possible because of the cramped space they have to work in. The closer you have to keep your chemical trays to the enlarger or the boxes of paper, the more careful you need to be. If you splash liquids you can ruin your work. Besides, you may not even realize in the dark that you have splashed around a few drops of chemical."

One entire side of his darkroom is a high workbench. The enlarger sits at one end. Shelves above the bench hold boxes of paper and cans of chemicals which he can locate even in darkness. The counter is kept cleared of most materials except when Bass is actually working there. This way he can set out only the materials he will need in the order he wants them. This means less groping around in the dark for what he needs, and therefore less chance of making a mistake.

The wet side of his darkroom has water piped in over a shallow sink. Racks above this developing and washing area hold the tanks and other equipment needed there. The faucet is a mixer type, so water temperature can be adjusted. A photo thermometer is fixed into the water line, so there is never a question about the water temperature.

Darwin Bass, like most serious photographers, has added his own refinements to his darkroom. Tongs hang where they are handy and always in the same place. High storage shelves keep extra paper and chemicals safely away from the work area. A foot pedal controls the light switch. Special small pigeonhole-type shelves store lenses where they are protected and handy near the enlarger. Tray shelves hold unused trays in a rack where they drain into the sink out of the way until needed again.

Here is a look at the essential equipment you will need if you want to develop and print your own pictures. Buy a roll-film developing tank made of either plastic or stainless steel. These tanks are made to fit the size film your camera uses. If you use more than one size film, you can purchase a tank with reels to hold different sizes. There are also tanks that hold two or more film reels at the same time. Tanks with large mouths have the advantage of filling or emptying faster than those with small openings. These tanks are filled and emptied by pouring liquids into them or out of them without taking the lid off. The liquids pass through a light trap. If the tank can be emptied and filled quickly, the film develops more evenly.

You will also need bottles for storing chemical solutions. These should be dark-colored containers. They can be purchased at photographic supply shops. Do not save and use bottles in which Clorox or similar materials have been sold, because these chemicals are extremely difficult to get out of the bottles. Glass containers are better than plastic. If they are light, they can be covered with black paper. Use waterproof labels or a grease pencil to mark each bottle for its contents.

In addition, before you begin to develop film, you will need a photographic thermometer, which has a long stainless-steel stem so it can be inserted into bottles and tanks of liquids. Timing the various steps accurately is so important in the darkroom that you should also invest in a photographic timer with large luminous numbers on the clock face and a timer bell.

You will also need clips with which to hang up freshly developed film for drying. These are available at camera shops, but wooden spring-type clothespins will work. The regular photo film clip is safer, however, because film can slide out of a clothespin. If it falls to the floor, it may pick up dirt or get scratched.

Also equip your darkroom with a sponge for wiping excess water from films when you hang them to dry.

In addition, you should have a large graduate or measuring cup for measuring liquids.

This takes care of the needs for film developing, except chemicals. Buy the chemicals recommended for the film you are using. These can be purchased in liquid or dry form ready to mix and with full directions. Chemicals needed include the developer and the fixer. You can use a plain water rinse between the developer and fixer, but it is less efficient than a stop bath.

PRINTING EQUIPMENT

Once the film is developed you have a negative. This is used to print a picture on paper. Light shines through the negative onto the printing paper and affects the silver particles in the emulsion. The variations of tone on the negative control how much light passes through. Where the negative is black, no light passes through, leaving the finished print white in that area. Where the negative is clear, enough light will pass through to print black. Various degrees of tone between these extremes will create corresponding shades of gray in the finished black-and-white print.

But exposing the printing paper to light is not enough. The results of the light's action on the printing-paper emulsion must be brought out by the chemical developer. In the dim light of your darkroom you can see the effect of the chemical solutions as they bring the picture to the surface of the paper. This is the magic moment when you begin to see the results of your work.

There are two basic kinds of printing. You can make prints the same size as the negatives; this is known as contact printing. Or you can enlarge the pictures by projecting light through the negatives.

You can make contact sheets by using a piece of clean window glass or plate glass. You may be able to buy it with the edges already smoothed. Otherwise, tape the edges to protect your fingers as well as to prevent scratching of film and paper. The glass is used to hold the paper and negative flat while exposing the paper to light through the negative. You can use a regular electric lightbulb on a cord or in a lamp that can be directed downward to make the exposure. If you have an enlarger, you can set up the negative and paper beneath it and turn the enlarger on to make the exposure. The length of the exposure depends on the negative density, kind of paper, and the light used.

A printing frame is somewhat easier to use. It is a frame fitted with a piece of glass and a backing board held in place by springs.

Another method is to use a printing box. This contact printing device is a box with light sockets built into it under a glass top. It is equipped with a switch so the light can be easily turned on and off. The simplest method, however, and often the best, is a sheet of plate glass.

As you become more deeply involved in photography you will doubtless want to make black-and-white prints larger than contact size, and for this you will need an enlarger. It will be the most costly item in the darkroom. The enlarger's job is to project the image of the negative onto the printing paper, much as a slide projector enlarges a slide picture onto a screen.

There are three basic parts to the enlarger: a strong lightbulb in a housing; a lens through which the light passes; and, between the light and the lens, a film carrier to hold the negative in position and keep it flat.

Depending on the enlarger, various parts are adjustable. Some have carriers that can handle only one size film. If you use a 35mm camera, you would buy an enlarger capable of handling negatives that size. Other enlargers can accommodate film holders of more than one size. The lens is adjustable so it can be focused. The height of the enlarger above the printing base, where the paper is held in position, is also adjustable for making prints of various sizes.

You should buy your enlarger with great care. If it has an inferior lens, it cannot make top-quality prints, no matter how good the lens on your camera. The enlarger is a longtime, maybe even lifetime, investment. You may be able to find a good used enlarger. If funds are limited, this may be a better solution than buying a lower-priced new one. But if you do consider a used enlarger, be sure all parts are in excellent condition, and satisfy yourself that the lens is sharp, clean, and free of scratches. If it vibrates—and many do—it is useless.

Some enlargers produce sharper images than others, and the reason is not always the lens. Select an enlarger that is equipped with a diffusing screen. The diffusing screen helps reduce the effects of dust, scratches, or other blemishes while still giving satisfactorily sharp images. Also investigate cold-light enlargers, which stay cool.

Before you begin enlarging photos you will need bottles for storing chemicals. You should also use five plastic trays for developing prints. These trays should be slightly larger than the largest prints you will be making. In addition, buy a pair of tongs for handling prints, an easel to hold paper flat beneath the enlarger, and a beer can opener for cans of chemicals.

Finally, you will need photographic paper. There are various kinds for use with negatives of different degrees of contrast. The standard paper for negatives with average exposure is number two. Paper comes in single, medium, and double weight, known as SW, MW, and DW. The heavier papers cost more, but do not roll and curl as easily. You also have a choice of surfaces on your printing paper. Some papers are glossy; these are the kinds generally used for magazine and newspaper reproduction. You can also buy paper with a dull finish known as mat, or one between glossy and mat, called semi-mat. There have been major improvements in photographic papers in recent years. The new resin-coated papers do not require as much washing and drying time as prints once did, nor must these RC papers be dried on stainless-steel surfaces to produce glossy prints.

19. WORKING
IN THE DARKROOM

ONCE YOUR WORK SPACE IS READY, you can begin the exciting business of converting your exposed film to pictures. The first step in this remarkable process is to bring out that latent image on the film emulsion, and this begins with loading the film into the developing tank. Because the film has to be put into the tank in absolute darkness, you may fumble with it at first. You can learn quickly, however, to follow the necessary steps. If possible, use a roll of outdated film for practice. This way you can watch the process a few times before tackling it in darkness with your good exposed film.

Experienced darkroom people will warn you about fingerprints on the emulsion side of the film. The emulsion is on the inside of the roll, and you must learn to protect its sensitive surface by handling the film along its edges as you push it into the reel.

Once the reel is loaded, slip it into the tank and secure the lid. After this step, you can work with the lights on. You may run into a problem, however. You want the film to develop evenly over its entire area, but the developer begins to work at once, and if it touches some areas of the film before others the film may be unevenly developed. The ideal is to expose the developer to the entire surface of the film at the same instant. For this reason, if you have a darkroom, it is advisable to fill the tank with developer before you insert the reel of film. Then drop the film into the tank and cap it. If you are working without a darkroom, it is a good plan to first fill the tank with water and soak the film a few minutes. Then dump the water and replace it with developer poured in through the lid.

Light-tight developing tanks, made of stainless steel or plastic, can be loaded in darkness, then brought into the light while the film is developing. (*Photo by the author*)

The film is held by its edges, bent slightly to curve its surface, then run into the spiraled channels of the spool, which fits into the developing tank. The tank is loaded in total darkness. (*Photo by the author*)

Before starting, be sure you have the chemicals mixed and ready to go. These come with full directions for both mixing and using them, and the directions may vary with the kind of developer used. The directions with the film will tell you which chemicals to use for developing. There are several developers, but the most popular one is D-76.

It is best to mix the D-76 at least a day before you expect to use it. The powder is first mixed to make what photographers call a "stock

For developing prints, the photographer needs a darkroom where he or she can arrange three trays for developer, fixer, and hypo. The bottles for the chemicals should be labeled. (*Photo by the author*)

solution." This can be stored until needed. The stock solution can be either mixed half and half with water or used full strength. Full-strength solution can be used again for a limited amount of film, but diluted solution should be used only once. Also, have the fixing solution or hypo ready to go.

You must think in terms of time and temperature, because both the temperature of the solution and the time it is in contact with the film are important. The developer should be kept as close to 68 degrees Fahrenheit as you can manage from the instant the film goes into the tank until it comes out. Check the temperature of the stock solution. The water you add to dilute it can be warmer or colder to help bring the level of the diluted solution to 68 degrees. It is a good plan to mix the developing fluid in a large glass measuring cup or graduate. You can adjust the temperature further by setting it in a container of hot or cold water and checking the temperature until it is correct. A mixer faucet is a convenience.

If the diluted developer is colder than 68 degrees, the film will need longer developing time; if it is warmer, less developing time is needed. The best procedure is to follow the manufacturer's directions to the letter, and the developing times for most kinds of film are listed on the developer container. When everything is ready, quickly fill the tank with developer.

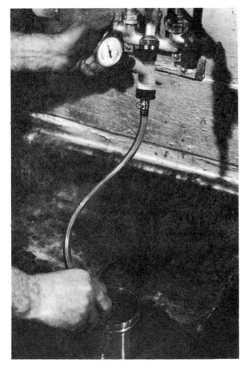

A thermometer on a kitchen mixing faucet helps to maintain the right water temperature during developing and printing. (*Photo by the author*)

Liquids can be drained off o. poured into the developing tank without removing the light-tight lid. (*Photo by the author*)

Once the developer is in the tank, it should be agitated every half minute or so. This keeps the developer working evenly over all the film. During developing, the tank can be kept in a tray of 68-degree water. Development may take from five to eight minutes, and the developer action should stop at exactly the time called for in the directions. This means pouring the developer off forty-five seconds ahead of full developing time. The chemical action will continue long enough to complete development.

To stop the action of the developer, pour in a "stop bath." This can be plain water. The temperature is no longer as critical as it was for the developer, but it is still a good plan to keep it within five degrees of the developer temperature. The stop bath should do its job in about twenty seconds.

After pouring off the stop bath, the next step is to pour in the fixer or hypo. The fixing bath's job is to remove from the film any remaining silver salts that might be acted on by light once the film comes from the tank. The container in which the hypo comes from the store will give the time needed for the fixing bath. During this process the liquid in the tank should be agitated as it was during development.

Then comes the washing, and this is also done in the tank. The film should be washed for about twenty minutes, and there are two ways this can be done. One is to dump and change the water in the tank every five minutes. The other is to let running water flow through it slowly by connecting a hose to the faucet and inserting one end into the tank. The tank can be open during washing.

Finally, the film has to be dried carefully. Fasten a clip to each end and hang one end from a line or wire. Then straighten it out and, while holding it this way, use a barely damp cellulose sponge to make a single, even stroke the full length of the film. This speeds drying and helps to remove spots and water marks from the film. Photographic stores sell detergent-type wetting agents which you can add to the final wash water to get a more even drying over the film surface. With a wetting agent the film should not be wiped.

While the film is drying, it should be in an area free of dust, because dust on the film can create spots on the finished prints.

Once the film is completely dry, you are ready to make prints. The printing paper, like the film in your camera, is coated with an emulsion of silver salts which are sensitive to light. You can tell which side of the paper is the emulsion side because it is shiny. With film it is the opposite: The dull side is the emulsion side. When you expose printing paper, the two emulsion sides should face each other. The dull side of the negative should face the shiny side of the paper.

An easy way to get acquainted with the printing process is to start by making contact prints. Let the enlargements wait until you better understand the steps involved.

First set out your five trays. These are for developer, stop bath, hypo (or fixing bath), second hypo, and plain water. These chemicals are not the same ones used for developing film. Avoid dripping materials from one tray into another. Instead of using water for the stop bath, use a solution of acetic acid obtained from the photo store. Temperature is less critical in printing than it was in developing; anywhere within the range of 65 to 75 degrees will be satisfactory. By using the safelight you can see your way around the darkroom as you work on your prints.

Contact prints are made by placing the negative right onto the

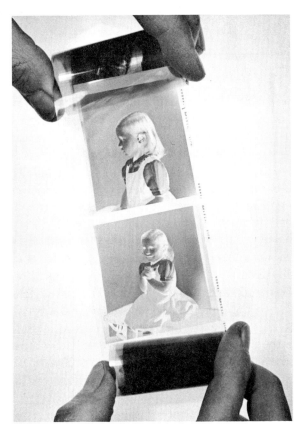

These quality negatives show good shadow detail and can be made into excellent enlargements in the darkroom. Slightly thin negatives are better than negatives that are too dark. (*Clarence W. Koch Photo*)

paper. Few negatives will lie entirely flat without a weight being placed on them, so use the sheet of heavy glass to hold them in place. The glass should be free of defects, clean, and dry. Printing frames and printing boxes are also made to hold the film and paper firmly in position.

When you have the paper, film, and glass ready on a smooth table-top, the next step is to expose the paper to light. You can do this with a 25-watt frosted lightbulb. Hold the light about three feet above the paper and, for a beginning, try an exposure of eight or ten seconds. Be sure the package of paper is closed before the light goes on. You may have to expose the paper for a longer or shorter period, depending on the density of the negative. The distance of the light from the paper also affects the exposure time needed.

Or you can begin with a test strip to help you find the best exposure time. With the paper, film, and light in place, expose the whole sheet five seconds. Then cover all but one strip of it and give it five more seconds of exposure. Each additional strip uncovered is exposed five more seconds. Once this test strip is processed, you can choose the exposure you like best.

The sheet of contact prints will help you determine which negatives will make the best enlargements. Many photographers shoot several exposures of the same subject, then select only the best for enlargements. It is easier to "read" contacts than negatives. You can also use the contact sheet to help you figure out how to "crop" a picture and print only the parts of a negative you want to see in the enlargement.

In addition, some photographers use contact sheets as a permanent record of their pictures and mark the sheet and each negative on it with a number corresponding to the negative they have on file. This way they do not need to sort through all their negatives and risk getting finger marks on them when searching for a picture.

Processing prints is the same whether you are making contacts or enlargements. Slip the exposed paper smoothly into the developer, emulsion side up, and be sure there are no air bubbles against it; then turn it face down. Rock the tray gently for a minute or two. Using tongs, you can then turn the paper over. At this point you can watch the picture gradually appear. Keep the paper under the developer, and every few seconds either move the paper or tilt the tray enough to agitate the liquid.

If the negative is a normal one, the print is properly exposed, and the temperature of the developer is 68 degrees, the print should develop in about one and a half minutes. Developing time may vary from this in either direction, but this is a good time to aim for, and if the print misses it by much, you will probably end up with a better print by remaking it at a different exposure.

Next, lift the print with the tongs and let it drain briefly over the developing tank, but do not keep it there too long, because the developer is still working. Then put it into the stop bath for about thirty seconds. Move the print or the tray constantly for the first ten seconds, then continue to agitate it frequently until the thirty seconds are up. This halts development.

After the stop bath the paper goes into the first hypo. Again it will require agitation, and this movement should be constant for the first ten seconds. Give it three to five minutes in the hypo, and move it around or tilt the tray every half minute or so.

At the end of this time, pick up the print with the tongs, let it drain a few seconds, then put it into the second hypo. Repeat the agitation given the paper in the first hypo, and leave it in this hypo for another three to five minutes.

If you use a resin-coated paper, these steps can be shortened. You will need only one fixer, and the fixing time is two minutes. This is because RC paper does not absorb chemicals.

Once the print comes from the second hypo, slip it into a tray of plain water and move it around a few times. Now you can examine the picture under strong white light and see how well you have done.

All that remains is to wash and dry your print. Prints should stay in the wash water for twenty minutes, and the water should be in motion. If you do not have a method for allowing the water to flow freely through the tray where the prints are washing, change the water every five minutes.

In this step also, resin-coated papers can shorten the darkroom time because washing can be finished in four to five minutes if the prints are agitated.

Prints made on standard photographic papers can be dried between large blotters with just enough weight on them to hold them flat. Here again, the new resin-coated papers can work magic and give you dry glossy prints in a hurry. All you have to do is sponge them off and lay them out on a blotter on a flat surface without anything on top of them.

In making enlargements, the only difference in this process is that you expose the paper by projecting light through the negative in an enlarger. This provides an opportunity to work with the negative and correct faults in composition or even in exposure. The enlarger will enable you to print any part of the negative. If you try to blow up too small a portion, however, the added magnification may give you a grainy print.

Before placing the negative in the enlarger, check it at an angle against the light to see whether it is free of dust. Dust on the negative will give you white spots on the print. Wipe the dust off gently with a camel-hair brush. The negative goes into the holder with the emulsion side toward the paper.

Next, put a sheet of plain white paper on the easel. The enlarger can be moved up to give you a bigger magnification, or down to make a smaller picture. You can move the easel so that only the portion of the negative you want to appear in the finished print is included.

Focus the enlarger carefully with the lens wide open. Then stop it down to $f/8$. Next, make a test exposure, using a one-inch strip from a sheet of printing paper to get exposures from five to fifty seconds, to

This set of two prints made from the same negative shows how cropping in the darkroom can improve a picture. The full-frame picture shows several points of interest to attract the viewer's attention. But by cropping out the ship and the foreground figure, the photographer has improved the picture of the two men and their canoe. These photos were made in the Galapagos Islands. (*Photos by the author*)

learn the best exposure time as well as paper to use for contrast for the negative. The test strip should include both highlights and shadows. Cover the strip with a sheet of cardboard, turn on the light for making the exposure, then begin exposing the test strip in sections at five-second intervals so the first section is exposed for fifty seconds and the last section for five.

Now turn out the room light, but leave the safelight on and exchange the plain paper for a sheet of photographic paper. Turn on the enlarger for the length of the exposure you have selected. Then put the exposed paper through the same steps you followed in making a contact print.

As you gain experience making prints, you will learn ways to do various parts of the process more effectively. For example, you can learn how to improve prints by "dodging." This is a system whereby you hold back part of the light from the projector while other areas of the print receive full light. It can be done with a disk of cardboard on a wire handle or even with your bare hands. A paper clip soldered to

A single picture can tell much about an event. This family is obviously on a canoe camping vacation and everyone is pitching in to get the camp chores done. With different lighting on the various faces, the photographer had to use the technique of dodging while making the print in the darkroom. (*Photo by the author*)

a piece of wire will take a variety of sizes of dodging disks. But it is important to keep moving the implement around so there are no sharp outlines of the dodged area. In this way you can darken sky, or foreground, or bring out the detail in a face without darkening the entire picture.

You can also "burn in" an area of the print by using a piece of cardboard with a hole cut in the middle. With this you can make the regular exposure as determined by the test strip, then give added exposure to the part you want to darken by letting the projector light shine through the hole while you move the card around. This is especially useful for darkening skies which are too light on the print. Or you can print the face on a portrait, then burn the areas around it until they are black, and in this way eliminate any areas that might distract from the main subject.

Once the new print is dry, you may find spots on it that are not part of the picture. These spots can often be avoided by more careful work throughout the darkroom process. As you put the negative into the enlarger, first check it for dust and use a camel-hair brush, or air from a squeeze bulb, to remove the dust. Impurities in water can make spots on prints; these impurities can be avoided by using a filter on the faucet.

But if there are spots on the print even after observing these precautions, you can still remove them if you are very careful in your work. The print may have either black spots or white spots, depending on whether the foreign material is on the negative or the paper. To remove black spots, use a single-edge razor blade to scrape the surface lightly. Another method is to use a reducer, which you can buy at the camera shop. White spots can be filled in by using a small brush to dot the area with colors from a retouching kit. The finished print, as near perfect as you can get it, is worth all the added work.

COLOR-SLIDE DEVELOPING

Most of us who make color slides have them processed at commercial color laboratories. This is the only choice if you use Kodachrome film. These rolls of film are sent to the Kodak processing plant in special mailing envelopes which can be purchased at photographic stores, and the results are usually excellent.

But if you want to try developing your own color film, you can use Ektachrome or GAF color-slide film and purchase developing kits for them. All directions for developing these films are included with these home-processing kits. Color processing requires somewhat more time than does black-and-white film, and greater attention to detail.

If darkroom work with color sounds interesting, you may want to also try making color prints. This can be done either by starting with a negative color film or by working from slides. To make prints from slides you can make an intermediate negative, then use this in the print box or enlarger with special color print paper. But there are also color papers available for making color prints directly from slides, and these eliminate the need for making a negative.

20. TAKE PRIDE

IN YOUR PHOTOS

A PHOTOGRAPHER HAS A RIGHT TO FEEL PROUD of a good picture. This is why we should do a better job of displaying the pictures we make. Too many photographers toss their prints into a shoebox or tuck them into an old envelope for storage.

A common way to keep photographs is in an album, and this is a good plan. The album protects pictures and keeps them from getting lost. It can also keep them organized. If you are a busy photographer, you may want several albums. These can be organized by subject matter, with one book for "Animals," another for "Friends," another for "Sports," or whatever other subjects you work with. You may then want to subdivide each book into sections and insert the pictures in the "right" place as they are finished. You can add pages to some albums as you accumulate more pictures. If your albums are organized to show pictures in a regular sequence, a chronological order, or to tell a story, they will be more interesting than albums where each page is unrelated to what comes before or after. The album is also a good place to record important information about each picture. You can include the date the photograph was made, subjects' names, the occasion, special photographic information, and other details. All this helps to make the album interesting and valuable. The notations should be uniform in treatment, either typewritten or written neatly in ink. It is also a good plan to assign each print a number.

This brings us to the question of how the negatives are kept, which may be even more important than how the prints are filed. Photographers often lose negatives. A few years later, if they, or one of their friends or relatives, want a new print of the picture, there is no easy way to get it.

Negatives should be kept dry and in an area where temperatures remain moderate. Usually any room in the house will do for this. But you should keep them in an order that helps you find one when it is needed. The file box does not have to be fancy. You can make a file. You may want envelopes for individual negatives or strips of them, and these are available at camera stores. Filing systems vary with the photographer. The important thing is to keep the negatives where they are dust-free and will not get scratched or damaged, and to have them in some order so you can find what you want. The longer you make pictures, the more important orderliness becomes as your collection of negatives grows.

Although the album and negative file may be all that is needed for black-and-white photos, some photographers will want to think about ways to display their most outstanding shots. Every photographer has a few pictures that please him and which he wants others to see.

Some of these deserve to be shown as large prints, perhaps 8x10 or larger. If you want to enter pictures in a competition or an exhibition, they should be mounted.

To learn about mounting pictures, start with a print you like. If you do the job carefully, the print will not be damaged, but if it should be damaged, you can always make another print from the negative. Obtain from an artists' supply store a piece of mat or mounting board large enough for the picture. This heavy cardboard will protect the print. Also purchase some dry mounting tissue, a thin paper with a dry adhesive coating on both sides. The adhesive is the kind that, when heated with an iron, binds two sheets of paper together permanently.

The dry mounting tissue should be larger than the print. Use a warm iron to stick the mounting tissue to the back of the print. A few light touches of the iron will do it. The next step is to trim both the print and the mounting tissue together; this is best done with a print trimmer. After this, the print and tissue are perfectly even and ready for mounting. Then position the print on the mat board in exactly the place you want it, carefully lift a corner of the print to get it out of the way so you can use the iron to tack down the corner of the mounting tissue to the mat board. Do this on at least two corners to hold the print in position for the final step.

The iron should be only medium warm and it should not be placed directly onto the photo. Instead, cover the print with a sheet of heavy wrapping paper. Then, when you are sure everything is in its proper place, touch the iron to one corner of the paper over the photo, and this should tack it in place. If everything is lined up the way you want it, begin heating the print by moving the iron farther and farther along it. Keep the iron moving, because you do not want the print to get too hot and wrinkle or scorch. When this process is complete, you have a well-protected photograph.

If you want to frame the picture or display it at a photo show, it should also be matted. The mat is another sheet of mat board or heavy paper mounted over the picture but with a hole cut in it through which the picture is seen. The mat can be fastened to the mount with gummed cloth tape. The hole is cut slightly smaller than

The photographer made this "out of the frying pan" shot to add a light touch to his set of camping pictures. (*Photo by the author*)

the photograph. If the photographer prefers, however, it can be cut considerably smaller or in any shape. In general, the most tasteful matting jobs are simple ones. The picture is what you want to display, and unless a matting job enhances the photograph, it should not be used.

If you make color slides you have a different set of challenges for keeping your photographs in order and showing them to people who want to see them. There are two ways to show color slides—by

This shot, made during a vacation in eastern Canada, records a scene seldom observed by visitors from other areas. (*Photo by the author*)

projecting them onto a screen, or by having color prints made from them. Many photographers like to keep prints of their color pictures, and these can be kept in albums as you would your black-and-whites.

Those you use for slide showings must first of all be sorted and studied. The worst mistake people make in showing their slides is to show every picture they have. Often there are several very much alike. The photographer has to make up his mind which of these similar shots he will show, which is a better exposure or better pose. This does not mean he has to throw out the rest. They can still be filed for safekeeping.

For this first sorting of your color slides, inspect each one with a magnifying glass, or by projecting them. As you edit your slide collection for showing, remove any that are not in sharp focus, that are duplicates, or that are unacceptable for some other reason.

The next step is to organize the slides you choose to show. Arrange them in logical sequence so they tell a story. A slide show should have a theme or subject; it should not be merely a collection of pictures that you happen to think are good photographs. Even if they are good pictures, there should be some other reason for showing them. A slide show can tell the story of a trip into the mountains or to the seashore. It might be a presentation showing a football team's preparation for a championship game, or it might cover the activities at a summer camp.

The slide show should be fast-paced, and the person who presents it should give some thought in advance to what he is going to say. You may even want to record your commentary to play with the slide show. If you approach the showing of your slides in this way, you will find that your audiences welcome your pictures much more than if you show them without sorting and without organization.

21. MAKE MONEY
WITH YOUR CAMERA

PHOTOGRAPHY IS SO MUCH FUN that most people who own and use cameras never think of making money by selling their pictures. But for those who want to make a business of photography, even a part-time business, there are opportunities in almost any neighborhood.

When Paul Mitchell, of Cincinnati, was preparing for his freshman year at Miami University in Oxford, Ohio, he faced a common problem: He needed money. Could he make money with his camera? He began to think about it. He owned a Nikkormat 35mm camera with a 55mm lens. This was not much camera equipment for anyone thinking of professional picture-making, but Paul decided that he was also a better-than-average salesman, so he began to knock on doors and to offer his services as a photographer of children.

He specialized in black-and-white prints. The first year they were 8x10's mounted in a simple white folder. But the next year he mounted them on a good grade of heavy cardboard and encased them in plastic. He also moved up from 8x10 to 11x14 mounted on 14x18 board.

He worked every day from nine o'clock in the morning till late in the afternoon, and there were days when he had nothing but turndowns. But he refused to give up. "There was seldom a week," he recalls, "that I did not have at least one job, and usually it was four or five."

Every aspect of an event, whether fishing trip or team sports, provides interesting picture possibilities. (*Photo by the author*)

On weekdays he lined up assignments. On Saturday he made his portraits.

The biggest problem was discouragement from the turndowns. "When they kept turning me down, I would get mad," Paul admits, "and then I'd work that much harder."

His pictures were made with available light, usually outdoors in a nearby park. He soon learned that the most popular poses were close-up head-and-shoulder shots. The next most popular was a three-quarter shot.

His aim was to pose the subject in front of a simple background, perhaps a wall with vines. But he wanted the background to be very dark in the completed pictures, and he sometimes burned the background in when working on the print in the darkroom. This minimized distracting elements so that the subject stood out better.

Shooting sessions generally lasted an hour, sometimes longer. He normally shot three rolls, and the last ones were usually the best because, by then, the subjects were natural and relaxed.

He allowed customers to choose the shots they liked best from contact sheets, and he delivered the finished enlargements within two weeks.

"I averaged about two hundred dollars a week," he says, "but it took a lot of hustling." For three years his photo business paid half of his college expenses.

He gave up the portrait business because it got to be the same thing over and over. But he did not give up photography. He has since purchased additional lenses and become more serious than ever about making pictures. Several years later he still gets occasional portrait jobs from satisfied customers who remember his work.

Other photographers become businessmen with their cameras while still in high school. Warren and Jeff Pence are brothers who attend the same high school and have a darkroom in their home. Whether the event is a football game or a homecoming dance, one of the Pence brothers is sure to be there with his camera.

Their pictures are used in school publications, but they have also done photographic assignments for local newspapers. Much of their business, however, is making prints for fellow students. If they make pictures of football players, cheerleaders, class officers, or the cast of a class play, they invariably have orders to fill for prints.

Not only does this kind of camera business mean good experience for a young photographer and earn some income; it is also an excellent way to become an expert photographer.

Other camera owners are doing similar work in every part of the country, with a single camera and one lens.

An imaginative photographer can turn his camera and darkroom to profit in numerous ways. Another idea the Pence brothers capitalized on is personalized calendars. This idea is workable in any darkroom with an enlarger.

These calendars are made with the help of calendar masks, which can be purchased for a few dollars at a camera shop. The mask has all twelve months of the coming year arranged with space to print in your favorite picture. The technique is simple. Cover the calendar section while projecting the picture into the space where you want it; then cover the picture area while printing the calendar part of the sheet. When you finish developing the exposed paper, both the picture and the months are there.

In this way you can turn out calendars with pictures of cheerleaders, a client's pet, a family picture, or any other photograph chosen as calendar art for the new year.

These make good promotional calendars to sell to local businesses, or personalized calendars for individuals. You may also want to give them to friends and members of your family. Calendar masks are available in various sizes and shapes.

If you have a command of basic photographic skills and are determined to find markets for your pictures, you can probably make money with your camera. Many people in your town probably need a photographer's services from time to time. Owners of small businesses sometimes need pictures for catalogs or advertisements. Newspapers will buy pictures with local human-interest angles. Real estate companies sometimes hire photographers. Successful commercial photographers become good idea people. They are always thinking about ways for customers to use their pictures.

GOOD PICTURES SELL YOUR WORK

If you want to do freelance photography, you will have to figure out a method for showing potential clients the kind of work you can do. Professionals carry a print portfolio, or a set of slides showing their top pictures.

The first rule is to select pictures that deal with subjects similar to those the client might want. If you are trying to sell your services to shoot a set of wedding pictures, wedding shots are what you should display. To sell baby pictures, show baby photographs. If you are calling on the editor of a trade journal or other magazine, take along pictures of subjects the publication covers: farm scenes for farm magazines; factory pictures for magazines directed to manufacturers or factory workers.

In the beginning you may not have enough good pictures for a portfolio. But you can shoot pictures specifically to help promote sales of your work.

MAKING GOOD NEWS PICTURES

Editors use thousands of pictures every day. They are printed in weekly and daily newspapers, trade journals, magazines, and school papers. Good editors do not use bad pictures if they can help it. Their pages have to compete with too many other publications as well as television programs. This means the pictures they publish have to be attention grabbers, they have to stop readers and make them take a second look.

All good news photographers know what interests readers most. Good news pictures show people doing something of interest. The camera catches them at work, or when their faces reveal strong emotions.

If you want to take good news pictures you must develop an eye for the unusual. A picture of a man walking down the street alone is usually not a good news picture. But a picture of a man leading an elephant down the street probably is. And a picture of an elephant walking down the street alone most certainly is.

Action is vital to good news pictures. If a farmer has invented a new way to harvest corn, do not shoot him posed, looking into the camera. Photograph him cutting corn. That's the reason for taking the picture—to tell a story. There are picture opportunities everywhere, even in the smallest towns. The photographer must learn to recognize them.

Photographers sometimes discover that they like darkroom work even better than shooting pictures. They become expert at developing film and printing pictures; and, if they want, they can turn these skills into money by doing darkroom work for others.

This was how Clarence W. Koch worked up a full-time darkroom business. Koch once clerked in a photo store in Cincinnati. Later he managed a darkroom for a local photographer who specialized in shooting pictures of children. Meanwhile he was continuing to work in his own darkroom at home.

Finally he gave up his job to set himself up in business at home. Professional photographers learned about the quality of his prints. Orders began to come to Koch's home from photographers and advertising agencies from many states, and pictures he printed appeared in the finest magazines. His darkroom ability gave him a profession he enjoyed and the opportunity to run his own business. Many other business opportunities can be found by photographers willing to search them out.

Millions of camera owners, however, will never sell a picture, and never care to. They have learned that photography can be fun, and this can be the best of all reasons for taking pictures.

INDEX

GEORGE LAYCOCK has written more than thirty books on natural history and conservation. He has also written several hundred articles for many national magazines, including *Audubon, National Wildlife, Reader's Digest,* and *Boy's Life.* When he writes of animals and the outdoors, he deals with subjects of lifelong interest. He is a native of Ohio, and holds a degree in wildlife management from Ohio State University. He has traveled and camped widely, gathering information and making pictures for his articles and books.